LEGENDS & FOLKLORE OF BRIDGEND AND THE VALE

GRAHAM LOVELUCK-EDWARDS

WITH ILLUSTRATIONS
AND PHOTOGRAPHS BY
JESSICA LOVELUCK-EDWARDS

Dedicated to Harriette, Jessica, Charlie and Joseph.

I have drummed these stories into you from an early age. Now it's your turn to carry the torch on to future generations.

Hopefully this book will help.

ISBN: 978-1913637-24-8
Printed and bound in the UK by
Severn, Bristol Road, Gloucester, GL2 5EU

Published by
Candy Jar Books
Mackintosh House
136 Newport Road, Cardiff, CF24 1DJ
www.candyjarbooks.co.uk

CONTENTS

Part II
Half Truths, Myths and the Supernatural

PART III
CUSTOMS, SUPERSTITIONS, AND MYSTERIES

PART IV
PLACE NAMES AND THEIR DERIVATIONS IN BRIDGEND AND THE VALE

INTRODUCTION

The counties of Bridgend and the Vale of Glamorgan nestle side by side on the South Wales coast between Cardiff and Swansea. It always comes as a surprise to people visiting the area for the first time that it is so beautiful. South Wales' recent history has been dominated by industry, so people expect to see coal mines and smoke belching from factory chimneys as far as the eye can see. The last thing they expect to find is thatched cottages, castles, dunes, a beautiful coastline and greenery.

It is an area steeped in history. The ancient megalithic burial chamber at Tinkinswood, near St Nicholas in the Vale of Glamorgan, is believed to be 1,000 years older than Stonehenge, and there are countless other structures dating back thousands of years dotted throughout both counties. It's not all about ancient history though; throughout the ages different pockets of this region have continued to thrive and develop economic and political significance. That is what gives this book such a rich seam to tap into.

You may be wondering what qualifies me to write this account. I have always been a history and legends geek, and from a very young age, the type of history that excited me the most was history I could touch and see, that happened in places I passed every day. I was also lucky enough to be brought up in a family of romantics, poets, musicians and storytellers who, in the Welsh bardic tradition (which I will expand upon more throughout this book) knew all the stories, legends, poems and folk songs about the area where I grew up; the area covered in this book.

There is a lot of ambiguity around some of the stories and events covered here. Like in a lot of rural areas, located far away from big cities and big events, written accounts, contemporary chronicles and unmediated representations of history are pretty thin on the ground. Most locals were not able to read and write, and outsiders had little reason to visit, let alone record their findings, for large patches of history.

We also have the Victorian era to thank for muddying the waters still further. Many of the great stories retold in this book were originally very old legends, passed down in the bardic tradition from generation to generation by word of mouth. Their subject matter appealed very much to a Victorian obsession with the ancient, the macabre, the supernatural and the romantic, something Charles Dickens tapped into with his *A Child's History of England*, which is much more of a story book than a history book. Victorian romantics are undoubtedly responsible for a bit of sensationalism, and for taking much older stories and reapplying them to newer subjects and people. R.D. Blackmore, the successful novelist and author of *Lorna Doone* is a case in point. As a young boy he had lived in what is now Porthcawl, and he employed his familiarity with both the area and its folklore in his novels, especially in *The Maid of Sker*, which is of course set on the coastline between Porthcawl and Sker House, near Kenfig.

This would be frustrating for pure historians, but for us it is a brilliant thing, because where historical fact has been lost, breathtaking stories and legends have been spun down the generations to fill in the gaps. Some of the stories captured here are small, little more than superstitions or old wives' tales particular to our corner of Wales. Others are big, the types of stories that would make front page headlines in the modern world. All of them, though, are fascinating and absorbing, especially if you know the places at the centre of them.

Where we have factual records, I have used them to add some historical context and perspective. I have also highlighted where narrative crosses over into symbolism, so you can see the hidden messages placed there by the bards to tell two stories in one. Through it all, I have tried my best to balance history and context with story value, rather than take the traditional historian line of denying everything for which I cannot source a reference. Here is a true story that best explains why I have done this.

A small boy was taken by his parents on a day trip to Stonehenge. All the way there he was itching to see the altar stone, where he had heard that human sacrifice had taken place. His mother (who, as a schoolteacher, should have known better) thought that the idea of human sacrifice might be a bit too scary for a small boy, so she went to great lengths to explain that it never really happened. What do you think happened next? Yep. From that moment on, he completely lost interest in the trip. Without that bit of excitement, it was just a day looking at old stones.

With that in mind, I have tried my best not to be a mood hoover, and hopefully I have used just enough historical fact to add some context and additional dimension without killing off any old legends.

These tales and mysteries have given me so much pleasure throughout my life. Now it's time for you to sit back and enjoy them too.

PART ONE

LEGENDS AND MYSTERIES BASED ON HISTORY

CAP COCH – THE MERTHYR MAWR MASS MURDERER

Let us begin with a spine-chilling true story. These events took place in the eighteenth century in and around an old coaching inn, in a sleepy cove near Bridgend. There's no use looking for the inn now. It was pulled down a long time ago. But it was the setting of some of the most grotesque events ever to have happened in Wales. They were the deeds of a local highwayman who went by the name of Cap Coch, which is Welsh for 'Red Cap'.

What do we know about Cap Coch? We know that he was lawless and something of a firebrand, with a reputation for being argumentative and aggressive, especially in drink. He was described by those who knew him as being of 'powerful build' with grey eyes, red hair and a bland face. It is believed that he spent some time in France and his red cap was worn as a symbol of unity with the struggle of the French revolutionaries. There is even a possibility that he fought alongside them.

Like many bully boys from history, Cap Coch did not work

alone. He led a gang of thugs who used the inn as their base. They would keep an eye out for travellers who might make good marks and hide in woods nearby to ambush them. Generally, they would prey on lone travellers, preferably ones whose ability to fight back had been suppressed by drink. They would give them a sound beating, then strip them of any possessions of value and leave them bleeding on the roadside as they made off with their booty.

The real bloodthirsty work, however, went on at the inn itself. Any merchant or seemingly wealthy traveller staying at the inn was likely to meet their doom in the dead of night, their possessions stripped and resold in Bridgend, and their bodies unceremoniously dumped in the neighbouring river at high tide.

Cap Coch and his henchmen are said to have grown opulently rich on this grizzly trade and continued in it for many years. In that time, it is not clear how many victims were killed. Some locals began to get suspicious when bodies kept being found at the mouth of the river in Ogmore-by-Sea, always at roughly the same time as packmen were reported missing while traveling through the area. However, the link was not made until after Cap Coch's death, when people at the inn discovered some of his stash of valuables and belongings, much of which bore the monogramed names of missing people. Even then, however, they had only seen the tip of a particularly gruesome iceberg.

In 1825, a bridge was constructed in Bridgend that was both strong and wide enough to take stagecoach traffic. This led to the principal route of the turnpike being re-routed through the town, something that helped Bridgend grow and prosper significantly. Up until then, all the stagecoach traffic ran past Cap Coch's inn, with passengers having to change there if they were travelling to London. This re-routing meant that the inn had suddenly lost its monopoly, and instead found itself isolated in what quickly became a rural backwater. As such, it ceased to be commercially viable and eventually fell into disrepair. By the beginning of the twentieth century the building was of more value as a quarry than a property in its own right, so it was ordered to be demolished. It was only when the building was pulled down that a cave was discovered. It ran off what used to be the old kitchen, and in it a haul of valuable personal effects had been stashed away by the murderous Cap Coch and his gang.

The matter was reported, and suspecting foul play, the local magistrate ordered that the surrounding garden be dug up to see what other secrets lay underground. What this unearthed was so foul it became notorious for generations. As soon as the digging had begun the labourers started to find shallow graves, each containing the skeletons of two or three bodies. The search continued beyond the confines of the property itself, into surrounding woods and fields. And the bodies kept coming.

Clearly Cap Coch had heeded the warning that people were getting suspicious of the bodies washing up downriver, so had switched to disposing of them in graves closer to home. It was a tactic which worked brilliantly for him, as despite his voracious appetite for murder, his guilt was not proven until eighty years after his death.

I know from personal experience that the story of his mass murder did not end there. I grew up less than half a mile away from where this all took place, and back in the 1980s some flood management work was done on the river Ogmore, at the point where the inn had been. I remember further human remains being found when a contractor's JCB sunk its shovel into the riverbank, and the area having to be closed off while the police investigated.

You may be asking what happened to Cap Coch. Did he get his just desserts? Reports from the time the bodies were discovered claim that he lived to the age of ninety and died peacefully in his sleep in 1820. However, there is more reliable, contemporary evidence that he was hung at Stalling Down, east of Cowbridge, for stealing a sheep. So, in some small way, retribution was delivered, even if fortuitously.

WHERE DID THESE EVENTS TAKE PLACE AND WHY WERE THERE SO MANY VICTIMS?

Up until the construction of the M4 in the 1980s, the principal, arterial route through South Wales has always followed the path of the ancient Roman road that ran between the forts at Caerleon and Neath. Much of this ancient road lies under what is now the A48. On a clear day, standing on the crest of the hill at Stormy Down looking east, you can see the outline of the original Roman road as it reaches the apexes of Broadlands, Crack Hill, Primrose Hill and Stalling Down. Some of it is modern road now, some of it is little more than a dirt track, and some of it has been reduced in status to byroad or country lane – but all of it, you can see, is dead straight.

The events of this story took place on just such a stretch. New Inn Road is a country lane which runs from Ewenny to the A48, opposite what used to be the entrance and driveway to Broadlands House. This particular stretch of road is well known locally, as midway along it is a rather celebrated fifteenth-century bridge known as 'the Dipping Bridge'. It gets its name from the archways in its south wall, through which sheep would be herded to be dipped in the river below. Even before the bridge was constructed, the river Ogmore was quite wide and shallow at this point, forming a natural ford, so undoubtedly it had been a crossing point for many years, possibly as far back as the original Roman road.

The left bank of the Ogmore by the Dipping Bridge was the site of the New Inn and many gruesome murders

New Inn Road gets its name from the old coaching inn that used to stand on the western bank of the river where the Dipping Bridge crosses it today. The inn was located on what is now a grassy bank. The road snakes around it after you cross the Dipping Bridge heading west, just before it turns sharply to climb the hill towards Broadlands. This is the exact point where the events in this story took place.

Up until the nineteenth century, in the golden age of coach travel, this route formed part of the principal road running between Gloucester and Carmarthen (and, indirectly, London and Fishguard). By the measure of its age, it was a very important and busy road, and commercially speaking, the location of the inn was a particularly good one. This crossing point of the river Ogmore was an important milestone for travellers, especially so for those on the stagecoach to London, who would have had to alight here and pick up a different stagecoach from Ewenny, on the other side of the river. No doubt many would have taken the opportunity to buy some refreshments at this point along their route. More significantly for the events we have been exploring, the New Inn would have been exactly one day's coach ride from either Chepstow in the east or Carmarthen in the west, both of which were significant market towns throughout pre-industrial history; in other words, the inn was perfectly situated for overnight stops. Moreover, in 1791 Bridgend made its first foray into the industrial revolution, with the construction of a huge woollen mill, drawing a steady flow of packmen carrying wool into the area. For these various reasons, a lot of travellers would have stopped at the inn or stayed there overnight.

WHO WAS CAP COCH?

Here's the thing about Cap Coch. We have accounts of how he dressed, why he wore a red cap, what he looked like and what he got up to. We even have some conflicting accounts of how he met his end. What we don't have is any conclusive evidence of his real name or where he came from. I have heard anecdotally that his first name might have been Will or that his surname might have been Williams, but I cannot find a source that backs up either of these claims.

Unfortunately, when Cap Coch was at large in the late eighteenth and early nineteenth centuries, public records were nothing like as substantial as they are now. The first UK census was not taken until 1801, and very little of that still remains. Even if more scrupulous records had been kept, it is questionable whether they would help us. During his lifetime Cap Coch covered his tracks so well, most people were completely unaware of his bloodthirsty goings on. All of what we know about him is drawn from accounts from after the event, from those who claimed to have known him.

SHIP WRECKERS OF DUNRAVEN CASTLE

The Bristol Channel is an especially treacherous waterway to navigate. It has a massive tidal range (the second biggest in the world, in fact) confounded with devilish cross-currents, impenetrably murky waters and numerous submerged hazards. It has never been somewhere for the faint-hearted to take out a boat. Even to this day, despite all their navigation aids and technology, the huge modern container ships docking in Avonmouth still need to hand control over to a locally licensed pilot to navigate the final stretch of their journey east of Barry.

The coastline between Porthcawl and Nash Point is especially dangerous. Beyond the estuary of the river Ogmore, little more than a mile out to sea, is Tusker Rock, a black, jagged rock that stays submerged below the sea line during high tide. Tusker Rock has torn open the belly of many a straying ship. As if that in itself were not sinister enough, it is also where the Schwyll (pronounced Shwill) Aquifer surfaces, a subterranean river that creates violent cross-currents in the estuary mouth. These have claimed many lives in my lifetime, let alone across the span of history. To the east of that is the Nash, a sandbank with the unnerving property of being able to move. An ill-fated ship called *Frolic* famously struck the Nash in March 1831, with the loss of seventy-eight lives, one of the worst tragedies ever in these waters.

To help seafarers steer clear of these terrifying death traps, in the nineteenth century two lighthouses were built. One was started in 1831, on the eastern flank at Nash Point, and thirty years later, another was built on the western flank at the end of the breakwater at the entrance to Porthcawl harbour.

Before these were built, night-time navigation along this stretch was mainly achieved by setting a course and keeping an eye out for the streetlights of Newton, in Porthcawl, which signalled that you were clear of the rocks. This was far from a scientific solution, and it kept the scavenging, coastal-living folk of the Vale of Glamorgan in a plentiful supply of plunder, washed up on their beaches from the wreckage of numerous merchant ships. Some took it upon themselves to unduly influence the number of wrecks, without any qualm or thought to the lives they were endangering in the process. With a tragic irony, the most prolific of these was a man who, in his earlier life, had sought to be the saviour of the victims of shipwrecks.

BRIEF HISTORY OF DUNRAVEN CASTLE

There has been a castle on the headland between Dunraven beach and Southerndown beach since the Iron Age. The earthworks for the original Iron Age hillfort are still visible (though best viewed from above) to the south of the later buildings. Legend has it that this was the home of Caradog (aka Caractacus, king of the Silures tribe, but more about him later). The name Dunraven may well be a corruption of the Welsh '*din-dryvan*', meaning 'triangular fort', which would describe the outline of the Iron Age structure quite aptly. The next castle to be constructed on this site was a twelfth-century fort built by Arnold De Boteler. In the mid-sixteenth century this was modernised and incorporated into a Tudor mansion, in much the same way as the Herbert family renovated the castle buildings in Cardiff Castle at around the same point in history. The mansion was eventually destroyed and replaced with a statement of Victorian fashion: a castellated nineteenth-century hunting lodge (similar in style to Crawshay Castle in Merthyr Tydfil), complete with folly in the grounds and ornamental garden. This was the seat of the earls of Dunraven, the Wyndham family, who also held extensive estates on the other side of the Bristol Channel in Devon and Cornwall, and in Ireland. It is the ruined remains of this later structure that you can see today if you visit the site. Apparently, this act of destruction came about as the result of a dispute with the local authority over planning permission. Largely out of frustration, the last owner of the castle demolished it in 1963.

Walter Vaughan and Mat of the Iron Hand

During the period we are concerned with here, in the sixteenth century, Dunraven's Tudor mansion was the home of the Vaughan family. This was recorded by John Leyland, a contemporary antiquarian and chronicler of note who visited the area. The mansion's situation, perched on top of the sheer cliffs of Southerndown, with its façade gazing out to sea across the treacherous Tusker Rock, made it the perfect retreat for a ship wrecker. But for Walter Vaughan things nearly turned out so differently.

Despite a promising start, Walter Vaughan lived a pretty tragic life. He was born into a very wealthy family, inherited the family estate, found a wife and was married and had children. He was a respected member of the community and served as a magistrate. Then things started to go wrong. He lost two (or in some accounts three) children in a tragedy at sea. As you would expect, he was distraught, and in some accounts, this was the catalyst for him to pursue setting up a sea rescue service, to make local navigations safer for seafarers. In other accounts, this idea came to him after he saw a ship in distress on the rocks and swam out to rescue survivors. Whichever is true, it is not altogether clear why the relevant authorities refused him permission to do this.

Not too long afterwards, his wife caught a fever, sickened and died. In a pit of grief, he turned to drink and gambling to dull the pain. As time went by, despite the cushion of his great wealth, things clearly got out of control, and he squandered away his family fortune, ending up with large gambling debts that threatened the loss of the family estate.

Outraged by this cycle of loss and depravity, and despairing that he had become unbearable to live with, his one surviving son left home to seek out his own fortune, and his daughter disowned him. Alone and threatened with financial ruin, he turned to an unlikely source for help: a local pirate, smuggler and ne'r-do-well who lived in the Broughton/Monknash area and went by the name Mat of the Iron Hand. This name he had earned on account of the iron hook that he had in the place of a severed hand.

Walter Vaughan gave Mat of the Iron Hand free reign of his estate, which spanned the clifftops east of the castle. It was on these clifftops that Mat organised teams to tie lanterns to the tails of grazing sheep, replicating the appearance of the lights of Porthcawl. Seeing these lanterns, passing ships would think they had passed the dangers of the rocks and would be lured onto Tusker Rock. The nearest beaches were also part of Vaughan's private estate, and Mat's teams would rummage unchallenged through the spoils and corpses washed ashore. Whatever they gathered would be split between Mat of the Iron Hand, his henchmen and Walter Vaughan. These wreckers, fearful that word of their trickery would get out, were absolutely ruthless. Any survivors who made it to shore were swiftly dispatched, to make sure their dastardly secret went nowhere other than the grave.

Walter Vaughan would send his servants to Southerndown Beach to collect the spoils from wrecked ships while he looked down from Dunraven Castle above.

Legend has it that Vaughan's life choices came back to haunt him. After some years, his son agreed to return home in a bid to mend their rift. In the time he had been away, he had travelled extensively and grown into an educated and wealthy man in his own right. A few weeks before he was expected home, there was a violent storm, and from his castle Walter heard a ship splinter against the rocks below. He sent word to Mat to send his cohorts down onto the beach the following day, to retrieve whatever had washed ashore. The haul they brought up to the house was one of the best they had ever seen. There was a great cargo and also some expensive clothes and valuable jewellery and art. Everyone was overjoyed, until Walter Vaughan, when rummaging through the jewels, found a ring that had been cut from the finger of its wearer. The ring had on it the family seal.

Walter Vaughan recognised it at once as a ring he had once given his son. He ran down to the beach, only to have his worst fears confirmed. There in front of him lay the body of his son, dressed in the finest clothes of the era. His throat had been slit from ear to ear. He laid lifeless and cold in the water.

I have also come across a slightly different version of this story, in which Mat of the Iron Hand lost his hand when an overzealous sheriff cut it off during a scuffle while attempting to arrest him for a misdemeanour. The arrest had been ordered by the local magistrate; yes, you guessed it, Walter Vaughan. In this version of the story it was many years later that their paths crossed again, when Vaughan was at his wits' end, looking for someone to bail him out of his financial troubles. Mat instantly knew who Vaughan was, but Vaughan did not recognise him and was oblivious to his own role in Mat's disfigurement. Mat bade his time, waiting for an opportunity to exact his revenge. It finally came on the day he found Vaughan's son washed up amongst the remains of a shipwreck on Dunraven beach. He was still alive, but the wreckers' code dictated that survivors had to be killed so plunderers could not be identified to the authorities. Thus, it was Mat who killed Vaughan's son, and cut off the boy's hand before offering his ring to his father – all in the full knowledge of what he was doing.

Whichever version we go with, there is no escaping that it is a rather neat ending to this story, and we will pick it up again later in this book when we look at reported apparitions, ghosts and hauntings (because there is no way a story this good could not lead to a related ghost story). In reality, this poetic ending compensates for a lack of contemporary historical fact. This is another story that became sensationalised a long time after the event. You are still able to read from the archives how it was published in *The Glamorgan Gazette* on 17th September 1859, nearly 200 years later, to quench the appetite of Victorian society for tales of the macabre, and also to maintain a theme that justice always prevails. Remember, this was an era when it was commonplace to re-write Shakespeare's tragedies so they had happy endings (as parodied by Charles Dickens in *Nicholas Nickleby*), such was the Victorians' desire for a good story to always champion order, balance and justice.

There is evidence to suggest that the practice of shipwrecking in the Vale was real and that the practise of tying lanterns to sheep did go on. There are reports of it being done by wreckers in Devon and Cornwall as well as in Wick and Dunraven. This was a more lawless time, so it could well have been common practice for landowners to allow servants and locals to plunder what they could from a shipwreck, and to cut them in on the booty. There also seems to be some unexplained improvement in Vaughan's personal wealth in later life. Also, as unlikely as the name Mat of the Iron Hand may sound, there are other references to him from that time, so the chances are he was a real person.

ROMAN TOWN OF BOMIUM

We have already mentioned the region's ancient Roman road earlier in this book: how in the Roman period it was the means of linking the forts at Caerleon and Neath, and how it formed the template for the region's only road for much of history. More recently it formed the outline of what is now the A48. In the period when the road was built, there was a Roman fort on the site of what is now Cardiff Castle. When the Marquis of Bute (a very keen amateur antiquarian and historian) rebuilt the ramparts of Cardiff Castle he took great care to make sure that the ancient Roman stonework was incorporated into his new structure. He ordered that it be highlighted with a frame of red stone, so it would be obvious to onlookers where the patches of original Roman stone masonry still existed. He also rebuilt the north gate of the castle in the style of a Roman gatehouse, after archaeologists discovered the remains of the original Roman gatehouse on that site.

Despite Cardiff's significance today as a capital city and the centre of Wales' politics and economy, in early history it was very insignificant. On the original Antonine Itinerary (a forerunner of what we might today call a road map) it was only noted as a fort, not as a town or settlement. In fact, the only settlement of sufficient note to be mentioned as a staging post was a place called 'Bomium' or 'bomio' somewhere in Glamorgan – but where?

The replica Roman north gate of Cardiff Castle, based on archeological remains found on its site. Something similar would have stood at the entrance to Bomium.

There are no records to prove it conclusively, but for several reasons it is most likely to be the town of Cowbridge. Firstly, it is linguistically likely that Bomium became corrupted to Bovium and from there to some cattle-related translation such as Cowbridge. Secondly, there is no doubt that the town is built on the course of the Antonine road. But the most compelling evidence is that Cowbridge has yielded a lot of Roman archaeology from the first century.

The most exciting discovery was a bath house which boasted tiles stamped 'Legio II Augusta' which would suggest the nearby presence of a military base. The fact that the bath house appears to have been destroyed after the Hadrianic period in the second century would support this. However, the discovery of this bath house raises more questions than it provides answers. First of all, the bath house was a very central part of Roman society. It was a place not just to visit but to be seen to visit. As such, pretty much without exception, they were located on the main thoroughfare of a town. The one in Cowbridge, however, is not only nowhere near the main thoroughfare, but it is also facing the wrong way. Was there another road cutting through Cowbridge that has been lost through time? It is possible; we also have the remains of some timber-framed buildings contemporary with the Roman period, the alignment of which would suggest this. But if there *was* another road, where did it go? The Romans didn't just build roads willy-nilly. It would have intersected the Antonine road from north to south. But there are no recorded Roman settlements for this road to have led to in either direction.

The other question raised by the bath house is that, if this was a military outpost, then where was the fort? Despite the many digs down the years – uncovering buildings and ditches behind the high street, coins and pottery from around AD 80, and some notable tomb monuments including an engraved stone lion – no remains have been found of anything that could pass as a fort. One theory is that it was located on the banks of the River Thaw and may have been demolished when the town moved from being a military post to an industrial hub. There is a lot of evidence to suggest that in the later Roman period the town became a centre of iron smelting, but how all these clues tie together is anyone's guess. Any evidence proving that Cowbridge is in fact the lost town of Bomium has long eluded local historians, and the mysteries continue to confound.

STRADLING'S LEGEND OF THE TWELVE KNIGHTS

Here is a legend that fascinates for any number of reasons. First of all, it's a good story full of feuds between kings, plots within plots, intrigue, treachery and murder. Secondly, it is the starting point of numerous spin-off legends. Finally, and quite significantly, it is fascinating because this story was at one time seen to be so inflammatory it had been banned in some quarters. People would have faced retribution simply for telling it. It also comes with far more contemporary historical evidence than most of the stories captured in this book.

A Brief History of Fitzhamon and the Norman Invasion of South Wales

The Norman conquest of South Wales was led by Robert Fitzhamon, the first feudal Baron of Gloucester. It is not clear when he first came to this country from Creully, in the Calvados region of Normandy. There is no record of him having fought in the Battle of Hastings, nor any reference to him in the Domesday Book of 1086 (although other members of his family are mentioned), so estimates put his arrival in Britain at around 1088. Whatever the truth, he first came to prominence during the rebellion of that year.

After William the Conqueror died, his two sons fought over the succession of the Kingdom of England and the Duchy of Normandy. Fitzhamon became a significant supporter of King William Rufus, who ultimately came out on top, and he was richly rewarded for his loyalty.

Before Fitzhamon's decisive victories over the local kings, there had already been a strategy to dominate and conquer south east Wales since around 1069. Occupation was maintained by the building of two castles at key river crossings, with motte and bailey forts constructed in Newport on the Usk River sometime between 1075 and 1080, and in Cardiff on the Taff around 1081. These strongholds were put under Fitzhamon's control when he was gifted his estate as Earl of Gloucester.

Fitzhamon then raised an army, with cohorts led by experienced, battle-hardened knights loyal to the king who had already proven their worth during the rebellion, the First Crusade, and a few as far back as the Battle of Hastings. The Welsh were well used to fighting amongst themselves, and with the odd Viking, but this was a force the likes of which they had never seen, and as such they were decimated.

If Middle Welsh is not your thing, this might be a good moment to introduce the two Welsh kings Fitzhamon defeated, and to give you an idea of how to pronounce their names and the names of their ancient kingdoms.

The first was Iestyn Ap Cwrgan *(pronounced 'Yes-tin ap Kurgan'),* King of Morgannwg (*pronounced 'Morgan-oog').* Morgannwg is essentially south east Wales, the area of land between the Severn Estuary in the east and Neath in the west. Iestyn's headquarters would have been somewhere near Kenfig. He had a running feud with his neighbour Rhys Ap Tewdwr (*pronounced 'Rees ap Tee-oo-doorr')* King of Dehaubarth (pronounced 'Dee-hawbath'), which was everything west of Swansea up to the tip of Cardigan Bay. His court would have been in Carmarthen.

> 1090 – Fitzhamon defeats Rhys Ap Tewdwr at the battle of Brecon. The king himself is chased from the battlefield and is caught and killed in Hirwaun.
>
> 1091 – Fitzhamon defeats Iestyn Ap Gwrgan. The exact location of the decisive battle is disputed but believed to have been somewhere in the Vale of Glamorgan. Iestyn flees the battlefield, takes refuge in the mountains of the Brecon Beacons and is subsequently granted land between the Neath and the Afon rivers provided he stays loyal to Fitzhamon.

The Welsh at this time were hell-bent on fighting each other, rather than uniting against a common enemy, and it is very likely that the Normans enlisted the support of Welsh princes, knights and warriors in both of these battles.

After defeating Iestyn, Fitzhamon sacked the deposed king's own castle at Kenfig, and round about 1100 built a motte and bailey fortification of his own on its site. This became the western frontier of the Norman kingdom.

To reward his loyal knights for these victories, and to maintain order on the ground, they were each given titles, a dowry and land in South Wales, with permission to raise a living from taxes, rents and managing their land. They were also given permission to build castles and maintain a fighting force of guards and soldiers. These knights were distributed as follows:

Sir William de Londres: Ogmore
Sir Richard I de Grenville (the younger brother of Robert Fitzhamon): Neath
Sir Payn de Turberville: Coity
Sir Robert St. Quintin: Llanblethian
Sir Richard Siward: Talyfan
Sir Gilbert Umfraville: Penmark
Sir Roger Berkerolles: St. Athan
Sir Reginald Sully: Sully
Sir Peter le Soare: Llanbedr-ar-Lai
Sir John Fleming: Wenvoe
Sir Oliver St. John: Fonmon
Sir William Stradling: St. Donat's

THE INTERTWINED LEGENDS OF THE CONQUEST

It is quite possible that Fitzhamon's motivation for this fight was nothing more than personal ambition, or an expectation that the king keep his subjects in check and loyal to the crown. However, the legends from the Welsh side give a more colourful explanation.

There was nothing the ancient kings and princes of Wales loved more than a good fight amongst themselves, and Iestyn ap Gwrgan and Rhys ap Tewdwr had been at it for years over a contested claim on some land.

The legend has it that Iestyn was getting frustrated at how long the feud had been running. Both sides were equally matched on the battlefield, neither side willing to back down, and there had been much bloodshed for very little gain.

So, after consulting his closest and wisest councillors, he agreed to send one of them, Einon Ap Collwyn (*pronounced 'Aye-non ap Col-win')* to meet with Robert Fitzhamon, earl of Gloucester, to ask for his help in defeating his troublesome neighbour. Einon was a natural choice for the job, as he was not only a knight who had proven his loyalty to Iestyn many times on the battlefield, but he was also himself of royal descent, the brother of Cadifor, the former prince of Dyfed who had been deposed by Rhys. Their family were well known to the English nobility, and there are even suggestions that Einon served William II when he was in France. Iestyn promised Einon that, if his mission was successful, he would grant him his daughter's hand in marriage, thus aligning their two royal households for life.

Einon met Fitzhamon and negotiated a deal whereby the earl would lend Iestyn the hired muscle of his twelve most trusted knights and their cohorts of soldiers in return for 'a mile of gold'. The two men shook hands on the deal and Einon returned to Morgannwg with his mercenary force in tow.

Buoyed by this vast tactical advantage, Iestyn threw down the challenge to Rhys to meet him in battle at Brecon. With Iestyn's own forces bolstered by the mighty armies of the twelve knights, he won easily, and Rhys' army was annihilated. In an act of cowardice, Rhys himself took flight, and Iestyn's troops pursued him all the way to Hirwaun, where they finally caught, trapped and killed him. It had been a great victory.

THE GOLDEN MILE

During the ensuing victory celebrations, the Norman troops marched to a mile-long section of the old Roman road and lined up in one long rank. Gold coins were placed side by side along the line of soldiers so that Fitzhamon would get his promised 'mile of gold', and the soldiers returned to Gloucester with their treasure. The stretch of road in question has ever since been locally know as 'the Golden Mile'. It is now the stretch of the A48 between the top of Crack Hill and Pentre Myrig in the Vale of Glamorgan.

There is some confusion about the legend of the Golden Mile, which I feel is worth clearing up.

The stretch of road my family called the Golden Mile ran from Bridgend to the foot of Crack Hill (past the Bridgend Ford dealership). However, at the base of Crack Hill, the Antonine road heads up into Corntown and Ewenny, rather than towards Bridgend, so this cannot be correct. Confusion over the exact route may have been compounded by the fact that there used to be a pub called the Golden Mile at the base of Crack Hill. It is now a Chinese restaurant called the Golden Well, and the name has latterly been adopted by another pub a few hundred yards away.

The other misinterpretation I have heard is that the Golden

Mile was a place where Roman soldiers would queue up (presumably in a queue a mile long) to get paid. This sounds very unlikely for a number of reasons. First of all, the obvious place to pay your legionaries is in a fortification where the paymaster is safe from robbery; somewhere the legionaries themselves are based. The nearest Roman fortification *might* have been in Cowbridge, five miles away, and if not, it was in Cardiff, twenty miles away. In the interest of security, it is very unlikely that enough money to pay a queue of legionaries would be transported out of a fort and distributed on a roadside where there was no protection. Secondly it is very unlikely that during the Pax Romana (the two-hundred-year peace within the Roman interior at its height) there were enough Roman legionaries stationed in the area to have formed a queue a mile long – although you could argue that depends on how far apart they stood from each other.

Backstabbing, Battle and the Bards

For Einon, the joy of victory in battle was short lived. He turned to Iestyn to remind him of his promise of his daughter's hand, but Iestyn denied having ever made such a commitment and refused him. Outraged that he had been duped, the broker of this victory – and the only one not to have profited from it – returned to Gloucester and asked Fitzhamon if he would join forces with him and turn against their former ally. Fitzhamon needed little persuasion. He saw a chance to gain wealth and land for himself. So Einon, Fitzhamon and the twelve knights returned to Wales and destroyed Iestyn's army in a fierce and bloody battle. They sacked his castle and court and, in the legend, killed Iestyn in the battle, although other records suggest he lived until 1093. This began the Norman occupation of South Wales.

In the retelling of this legend by the Welsh bards, Einon was always portrayed as a traitor who laid his own country open to attack from foreign invaders for his own benefit. A lot of folklore has spun out from that. One of the more colourful stories tells the tale of a drover who was herding his cattle through the Vale on his way to Smithfield Market in London (a common practice throughout the middle ages). He is said to have taken a nap under a bush and woken to find an old grey fox staring down at him with a pained and anxious facial expression. Before the drover could shoo him away, the fox spoke, pleading for the drover's help, explaining that it was the spirit of Einon ap Collwyn, who had betrayed the Welsh to the Normans and as a punishment was doomed to spend the rest of eternity as a fox.

The bards used to love to tell a story within a story, and frequently injected their tales with hints to ancient but familiar Celtic legends and superstitions which their audience would have understood – in particular to make it clear which characters you were meant to like and which were the baddies. There are lots of Welsh country tales, no doubt based on ancient Celtic and druidical traditions, in which the fox is a symbol of dark magic and deception. There is one such story in which a fox is an agent of the devil, sent to spy on mortals and report back with their weaknesses. There is also an old superstition in South Wales that seeing a grey or white fox means an imminent death in the family. We will look more at these superstitions later in this book.

*

WHY THIS LEGEND WAS DANGEROUS

In reality, no one at this time would have identified with the idea of Wales as a single entity, and this leads us to the thorny issue of the political subtext of such legends.

St Donats Castle was built by Sir William Stradling on land gifted by Robert Fitzhamon. It was a reward for his part in conquering the kingdom of Morganwg. His descendent Sir Edward Stradling wrote up the legend of the twelve knights we know today.

The legend of the twelve knights was first recorded by Sir Edward Stradling of St Donats Castle in the Vale of Glamorgan. He was a celebrated historian and antiquarian of his day and kept an enviable collection of ancient texts in his library at St Donats Castle. In 1571 he wrote an account of the Norman conquest of South Wales as led by Robert Fitzhamon, entitled *the Winning of the Lordship of Glamorgan out of Welshmens' Hands*. The story catalogues the battles and events of the Norman campaign and draws evidence from contemporary records and Welsh folklore. It goes on to tell the story of how Glamorgan was then ran by twelve knights loyal to Fitzhamon, all of whom were real people, one of them Stradling's ancestor. Many of the others, meanwhile, were the ancestors of his personal circle of friends, which is perhaps not surprising considering his aristocratic status.

So, historically accurate? In patches, without a doubt, and all of it is at least possible, even probable. But undoubtedly the narrative draws on the writer's imagination, though it is hard to say how much.

Particularly suspect is the emphasis on there being exactly twelve knights. We know from contemporary records that far more than twelve noble families were given land and estates in Glamorgan after the invasion. But twelve is exactly the same number of knights who sat at the round table at the court of King Arthur at Camelot, and, of course, the same number of disciples who sat with Jesus at the last supper. It is, perhaps, a more satisfying number when it comes to the spinning of a good yarn.

The two-hundred-year period culminating in the seventeenth century was an age of cultural enlightenment amongst the gentry. The renaissance had been sweeping across Europe, celebrating everything classical, and stories of King Arthur and his adventures with the knights of the round table became a staple of the movement after William Caxton published Sir Thomas Mallory's *Le Morte d'Arthur* in 1485. From then on, they were frequently the subject of tapestries, paintings and frescos across Europe. No doubt, Stradling's emphasising of the twelve knights was intended to capitalise on this.

Even though it had not been published in English until Stradling's time, the legend of the twelve knights was very well known in Wales. It had been re-told through the bardic tradition of story, song and poem down the ages since the twelfth century. However, during the fifteenth century this story had become something of a rebel's charter, a favourite of the nationalists Owain Glyndwr led in rebellion against the English lords in Wales. When Glyndwr died in 1415, he gained almost mythical status in the eyes of those he had inspired, and with one of his direct ancestors a central character in the twelve knights legend, the English establishment of the time saw it as a very dangerous tale to tell.

Did Stradling have a political agenda when he put pen to paper? After all, he was a prominent political figure of his day. He had been an MP on two occasions and sheriff of Glamorgan for many years. Was he deliberately stirring up Welsh nationalist feeling by bringing to the fore this subversive, nationalistic Welsh story?

The chances are that igniting Welsh nationalist fervour was not his driving motivation. In reality, the nationalist cause of Glyndwr's time was led by Welsh lords who were being disenfranchised by the English nobility, finding themselves out of favour with the English court. All that started to change in 1485, when the Pembroke-born Henry Tudor took the English throne, helped on his way by many of these Welsh lords. Once in power, to reward their loyalty, Henry gave them land, titles and top jobs, and this continued throughout the Tudor dynasty, until Elizabeth I died in 1603, thirty years after Stradling had written his book. At Stradling's time of writing, then, the Welsh nobility had much to be grateful for, and the sting of the story had been lost.

In all likelihood, Stradling's retelling was just a long overdue effort to capture the story in writing for the enjoyment of future generations. No doubt it also would have done his social standing no harm to compare his antecedents with the legendary knights of King Arthur and the round table. It is quite likely that he would have believed his family's reputation needed a bit of rehabilitation, since his father, Thomas Stradling, had found himself on the wrong side of the law when he had been arrested for illegally selling religious artefacts. A claim to be descended from a legendary knight would be one in the eye for all the curtain twitchers who might have relished the scandal, about which there is more later in this book.

LOST CITY OF KENFIG

If you visit the serene waters of Kenfig Pool, or the surrounding dunes of Kenfig Burrows Wildlife Reserve, it is difficult to picture this place as having ever been the site of a thriving conurbation. But my father used to tell me the story of 'the lost city' whenever we would walk across the dunes to Sker beach.

I can confirm that there is bounteous historical and archaeological evidence supporting my father's tale. From the eleventh to the fourteenth century, there was a thriving town, port and merchant population here in Kenfig. Any claim of city status may be dubious, but let's gloss over that for now. Not only do we know there was a settlement, we also have a lot of information telling us about the place.

But first, let's deal with the obvious question: what happened here? A whole thriving town lost, quite literally, to the sands of time. No trace of it left, just a wide, still, black lake, impassive dunes, and an eerie silence.

I can offer two explanations, so let's start with the more entertaining one.

*

The inky black waters of Kenfig Pool, said to be the watery grave of the lost city of Kenfig.

THE LEGEND

By the fourteenth century, the land making up the old county of Glamorgan was the estate of the De Clare family, high-ranking nobility of Norman decent who were the earls of Glamorgan.

One day, a peasant living in Kenfig saw the daughter of the great earl and declared his love for her on the spot. But knowing that a union in love with a peasant boy was impossible, she refused him. Before they parted, however, she gave him her silk glove as a 'favour', so that he knew that she secretly reciprocated his love.

This was a desperate plight for a young peasant boy with no money or prospects. He tried to think of ways he could prove himself worthy of winning her but could think of nothing. Then he hatched a dark plan.

He went to visit a noble knight, who had fought in ancient wars but was now old and frail and had dedicated his life to God. The peasant boy asked the old knight to lend him the trappings of a rich man so he could convince his love that he had succeeded in amassing a fortune. But the old knight would not hear of it and scolded him. He warned the boy that winning a bride by deception was no basis for love, and that he would come to regret his actions when the truth was inevitably discovered.

The young boy, hot headed and fuelled by passion and lust, could not cope with the uncomfortable truth of the old man's wisdom. In a fit of temper, he slashed out at the old man with his trusty sword. Though old, the blade was still razor sharp, so with a single blow the boy cut the old knight's head clean off. To cover his tracks, he tossed the old knight's remains into a nearby lake and helped himself to his money, fine clothes and riches. He paraded himself before the earl and his daughter, claiming the old knight's fortune and lineage as his own.

The girl and her father were very impressed, and she agreed to marry him. They were married in the Church of St James in Kenfig and had a great wedding feast in the old Guildhall. Just as the festivities were getting under way, the ghostly voice of the old knight rang through the rafters, calling out, 'Vengeance will be mine!' The terrified guests ran in fear but the boy, in the knowledge that he had incurred this wrath, stood fast. He asked the ghostly voice, 'When will this happen?' and the reply came, 'Vengeance will come with the ninth generation.'

When he told the others of this they just laughed and said, 'In nine generations' time we will all be long gone!' But they had misinterpreted the threatening words, and when a child was born soon after, the locals were oblivious to the fact that he was the ninth generation to be born in the town of Kenfig. The voice echoed once more, threatening, 'Vengeance will be mine!' Terrified, all the people of the town ran to their homes and bolted all their windows and doors.

But to no avail, for suddenly a huge tidal wave rushed in from the sea, up the river Kenfig, and completely engulfed the town, obliterating all its fine buildings and depositing a wall of sand to keep the lake from ever draining. All the inhabitants were drowned, and the only sign that the town had ever been there were the chimneys of the houses, still smoking above the water line. On the shore were found the gloves of the old knight, which washed up by the feet of a young descendant. As they were discovered, the voice of the old knight was heard from the sky praising God.

The legend has it that, on a clear day, when the water of the lake is still, you can still see the houses at the bottom of it. And if you listen carefully, you can occasionally hear the bells of the old church still ringing, warning of an approaching storm.

THE HISTORY OF KENFIG

As we covered in the previous chapter, the Norman conquest was a bloody affair, and as you would expect, displaced locals did not take kindly to having their land confiscated by the invaders. Skirmishes and backlashes were commonplace in all areas, but in particular in Kenfig, the former seat of the deposed King Iestyn. The town was soon established as a Norman enclave within the otherwise precariously held western flank of Norman-controlled Wales, and it was a frequent target of disgruntled Welsh retribution. It is amazing it survived its early years at all.

A stone keep was soon required to strengthen the motte and bailey that had replaced King Iestyn's castle. Lower ranking Normans were encouraged to settle within the protection of the castle and build their own communities. Wales' conqueror, Fitzhamon, intended to make Kenfig South Wales' commercial and industrial hub – meaning that he would control the entire local economy. An early description of the town refers to it having a port on the banks of the river Kenfig, which means that the course of the river must have been quite different to today. It also means that Fitzhamon controlled the area's sea trade, pulling income away from nearby Neath.

Surrounded by a deposed king, displaced landowners and disenfranchised seafarers, it is hardly surprising that the town suffered regularly from raids. In fact, records suggest that it was burned down so often that inhabitants built a stockade around the perimeter – only to have this struck by lightning and burn down as well. But this is not what devastated the town.

As time went by, the sieges began to lessen in regularity and the town prospered, becoming a significant trading post. Welsh as well as Norman inhabitants poured in, looking to make their fortunes in the town's blossoming trades and markets. Its burgesses were given a charter allowing them to levy taxes and pass by-laws. We have on record that they used this authority to set high standards in regard to the quality of food and drink produced and sold in the town, and around the cleanliness of the streets. They had a town hall, a guildhall, a hospital, a church and master measures to ensure fair weights and measure. They had strict rules against gambling and fighting. They had the right to hold fairs, and every November threw 'the Mabsant', a celebration of their patron saint and benefactor.

So what went wrong? Rather than raids or ghostly vengeance, it was Mother Nature who decided the fate of Kenfig.

A series of terrible storms in the fourteenth century regularly caused the marshland surrounding the town to flood, and eventually this led to the beginnings of the now seventy acre lake that we today know as Kenfig Pool. So, was it this that caused the flooding of Kenfig? Alas, stories of the town being at the bottom of the lake are a romantic invention. It makes for a cracking legend, but in reality the old town was located quite a bit to the north of the lake, pretty much alongside where the London to Swansea railway line is today. So, if it's not under the lake, why did the town disappear?

These storms brought in a lot more than just torrential rain. They also blew in a lot of sand, which soon started to form dunes. The problem with ingressing sand is that, once it takes a grip, it is very difficult to stop, spreading a little bit further every day. With the prevailing westerly wind blowing in relentlessly, sand soon got into everything. Gardens could not be cultivated, streets were constantly blocked, commerce became impossible. Areas of the town that were in the path of the dunes were abandoned, leaving only a small number of dwellings on the higher ground, which remain there to this day.

By the time the sixteenth-century chronicler Leyland visited the place, he described it as 'a little village on the est side of Kenfik and a castel booth in ruine and almost shokid and devoured with the sandes that the Severn Se there castith up'.

These sand dunes also wiped out a few other villages along the coast, such as Treganllaw and Candleston. You can still see the remains of some of the buildings out on the dunes that run between the Merthyr Mawr estate and the sea.

THE SECRET CULT WHO LEFT THEIR MARK IN PORTHKERRY

Here is something of a mystery from the picturesque little church of St Curig in Porthkerry, Vale of Glamorgan. It's not a particularly famous church, and it lies hidden away in woods. Most people do not even know it's there. To get there from Porthkerry Park you had best go on foot and climb through the woods on the western side of the park, near the viaduct. I must declare a personal interest at this point, as I have the privilege to be a church warden here.

As you walk towards the heavy oak door of the church, you cannot fail to notice some scratches and engravings in the timbers. This ancient graffiti is a clue to a chapter of our local history that reads like a Dan Brown novel. It is proof that an old and secretive cult was once rife in this corner of the Vale of Glamorgan, and that its members were not afraid to put two fingers up to the church establishment, even if in the subtlest of ways.

This all dates back to 1534 and the reformation in Britain, when Henry VIII declared himself the head of the Church of England. As has been well documented, not everyone was happy with this arrangement, but one of the lesser known pockets of resistance was a movement called the Marian Cult. They had one overriding problem with the reformed church, and that was the downgrading of devotion to the Virgin Mary. By 1552 the Book of Common Prayer was stripped down to just three mentions of her, and this was too shocking for some. So it was that the Marian Cult (most of whom were respected craftspeople such as carpenters and stonemasons) would meet in secret, to continue worship that featured devotion to the Virgin Mary as a central theme.

Eighteenth-century graffiti carved into the church door at Porthkerry reveals an ancient and secretive cult was once rife in the area.

Despite the secretive nature of the cult, they were not afraid to display signs of their defiance. What appears to be a 'WA' carved into the door of St Curig's is a point in hand. This is a symbol with numerous interpretations. In its simplest interpretation it is an inverted 'M' for Mary. However, in its inverted form it is also two V's to denote 'Virgin of virgins'. And lastly, of course, where the lines meet, they form a cross; no prizes for guessing what that means. The 'A' is an abbreviation of 'Annos', the Latin for 'year', and below you can see the year '1790'. This symbol was widely used to allow fellow cult members to identify where they might find likeminded worshipers.

Not all symbols were quite this crude. As many of the members of this cult were craftspeople, they often left their mark in more indelible ways, in the actual fabric of the church building itself. Often you will find a subtle engraving on a doorframe or in a hidden corner; however, it seems the cult members in Porthkerry grew pretty brazen in their defiance.

As you enter the church, directly facing you is a seventeenth-century memorial, and in the top left hand corner an engraved rose with open petals. This was also a symbol of the cult, and its presence on this tomb tells us either that the noble family remembered there were members, or (more likely) that the stonemason who engraved the memorial saw an opportunity to put the mark of the cult in plain view. No doubt this would have marked him out as something of a legend to his fellow cult members, who would have seen it every time they went to church, knowing that those outside their circle remained completely oblivious to its significance.

These two symbols also indicate that the cult was able to thrive in this area for a pretty long period. No doubt it would have been established when the cult was at its height nationally, in the late sixteenth century. However, the memorial is dated twice, and both dates are in the seventeenth century; the marking on the door, meanwhile, is dated 1790. In other words, potentially the cult endured for over 200 years.

This is quite unusual. The cult is not generally thought to have survived for such a long period elsewhere in the UK. It did enjoy something of a revival in the eighteenth and nineteenth centuries, with the rise of the Oxford Movement, an attempt by scholars of various university colleges in Oxford to introduce more Roman Catholic thought and practice to the Church of England. But could that have resonated in faraway South Wales?

For us the mysteries remain. Who were the daring engravers who left their mark on the church? And how did the cult survive so long without retribution?

SMUGGLERS & PIRATES OF THE GLAMORGAN COAST

Despite generally being brutal and murderous outlaws acting out of greed and malice, for some reason pirates hold a fond place in the hearts of many. And it's not simply a recent thing that you can attribute to Jack Sparrow. It has been going on for centuries, with the likes of Long John Silver and the privateers of the seventeenth-century Anglo-Spanish conflict revered as folk heroes. The same seems to be true of smugglers, with the eighteenth-century poet and essayist Charles Lamb writing, 'I like a smuggler, he's the only honest thief'.

The age of peak lawlessness on the seas was during the seventeenth and eighteenth centuries. The concept of charging excise duty on imported goods, imposed by customs officers employed by the Crown, only started in the seventeenth century. As you would expect, it was not a popular reform. Suddenly imported goods rocketed in price, as merchants had to cover the additional cost of getting their goods to market.

Even though we as a nation were nothing like as reliant on imported goods back then as we are now, the goods that were most affected were special treats and luxuries, like tobacco, sugar, wines and spirits, spices and exotic materials like silks. Once imposed, these duties continued to rise for around 100 years, and that created a huge incentive for smugglers to import goods in secret (or for pirates to steal them) and avoid paying the duty, allowing much lower prices than legitimate importers.

The other factor that made these lawless activities so appealing were the series of wars between Britain and the Dutch, the Spanish and the French. When Britain was at war with a foreign nation, raids on that nation's ships were seen as fair game. At this point in history, all three nations were plundering great amounts of wealth and treasure from their colonies, and with their waters within striking distance of Britain, everything from gold and precious stones and metals to spices and tobacco flooded the black market.

It is always going to be very difficult to legitimately obtain goods from a country you are at war with. For example, when Britain was at war with France, it was illegal to buy French brandy. So even if you had acquired French brandy perfectly legally before the war, the only way it could be sold was through the smugglers' black market. The authorities, determined to stamp these activities out, took smuggling very seriously. In fact, it was a capital crime, and those convicted would hang until they were dead.

Having a coastline as glorious as ours, it will come as no surprise that we have given the world some great seafarers – and as you might also expect, they did not always live on the right side of the law.

South Wales' most famous pirate (or privateer) was of course Sir Henry Morgan, a rather brutal swashbuckler, now immortalised by the drinks company Diageo, who decided to name a brand of rum after him (Captain Morgan). He is also said to be the inspiration behind the author Rafael Sabatini's novel *Captain Blood.* He was born either in Rumney on the eastern side of Cardiff or a few miles further east in Pencarn, which was on the mouth of the river Ebbw between Wentlooge and Newport. We don't want to dwell on him too long, as he was neither wholesome nor local, but I feel he is at least worth mentioning, as his career truly epitomises the rewards and renown piracy could bring. His exploits earned him immense wealth, a knighthood and the esteemed position of Lieutenant Governor of Jamaica.

He might have taken the pirate life to the extreme, but there were countless others from Bridgend and the Vale who (to borrow from the advertising slogan) lived like the Captain.

Earliest raiders

The earliest accounts of raiders on our shores date back to the fourth century, when we were the frequent target of Irish and Pict marauders. We don't know much about these raids, other than early monasteries in the area were usually the target.

In the ninth century, we also suffered at the hands of the Vikings. There is not much Viking-based history in South Wales, especially when compared with the east coast of England, Scotland, Ireland or even the north and west coasts of Wales. That may seem strange, especially when you consider that, just a few miles up the road, the city of Swansea was established as a Viking settlement by Sweyn Forkbeard, who went on to be a Viking king. (The name 'Swansea' is believed to be a corruption of the Norse '*Svyeinsy*', meaning 'Sweyn's island' or 'Sweyn's inlet'.)

There are a few reasons why there was comparatively little Viking activity between Swansea and Cardiff. The first is that their fairly rudimentary navigation techniques were not up to overcoming all the treacherous hazards of our waters, which we have already spoken about in an earlier chapter. The other, more substantial (and somewhat embarrassing) reality is that there was not a lot here worth plundering. However, there must have been sufficient that the Vikings did come and raid here on occasion; we have the place names to prove it.

One is the not especially imaginatively named 'Tusker Rock': '*Tusker*' translates as the Norse word for 'big rock', so when we say Tusker Rock, we are in fact saying 'Big Rock Rock'! But perhaps the most well-known is Steep Holm, an island in the Bristol Channel, off the coast from Lavernock Point in the Vale.

'Holm' is an old Norse word describing a fort or base camp surrounded by water, as in the Swedish city 'Stockholm'. The Holm islands – Steep Holm is just one of many 'Holms' all around the coasts of Britain – got their names from the Vikings' use of them as staging posts for devastating raids on the mainland. In 984, it was documented that the Vikings had set up camp on Steep Holm, and from there they devastated the north Somerset shoreline. In particular, a lot of carnage, destruction and loss of life was reported at Watchet and Porlock. They also attacked the South Wales coastline, focussing mainly on Llantwit Major and the monastery at Llancarfan.

PIRATES OF THE SIXTEENTH AND SEVENTEENTH CENTURIES

As South Wales began to grow prosperous in the sixteenth and seventeenth centuries, ports sprung up all along the coast to ship our produce to market. They included Newton in Porthcawl, as well as Aberthaw and Penarth in the Vale. Even Cardiff began the expansion that would one day see it grow to be the second busiest port in the world. These ports traded mostly with their counterparts in north Devon and Somerset, but often also further afield. All this nautical activity acted like a magnet to a rash of pirates who operated off our coasts.

COLYN DOLPHYN

Colyn Dolphyn was originally from Brittany, France, and operated out of Lundy Island. He was described as a tall, athletic and mighty man, 'like Saul in Israel'. He 'towered head and shoulders' over the Welsh and English alike. Colyn Dolphyn's name struck terror into the hearts of sailors in the Bristol Channel, where he picked off cargo ships with startling regularity.

He could never have known his luck one night in 1449, when on board his ship *the Sea Swallow*, his lookout spotted a boat on the horizon, sailing from Minehead towards the South Wales coast. It seemed to be alone and running low in the water – a tell-tale sign of a heavy cargo. Dolphyn and his crew caught it, pulled up alongside and boarded, only to find that the most valuable item on board was not its cargo. It was carrying a passenger whose name may sound familiar to you: Sir Harry

Stradling. He was the son of Sir Edward Stradling, historian and author of the legend of the twelve knights, lord of St Donats Castle, justice of the peace and chamberlain of South Wales.

Seizing this outstanding opportunity, Dolphyn took all the company of the ship prisoner, including Sir Harry Stradling and his trusted companion Derwyn. From the safety of his stronghold on Lundy, Dolphyn demanded a ransom for Stradling's release: 2200 marks, a massive sum of money for the time. It took Sir Edward Stradling two years to raise the money, and he was forced to sell multiple manors and estates, including those at Bassaleg and Rogerstone, Gwent, to do so. But he did finally pay off Dolphyn and got his son and his traveling companions home safe and sound.

Some time later Dolphyn was caught in a storm and his ship ran aground on Colhugh Beach in Llantwit Major. Hearing of the sighting of his ship, Sir Harry Stradling and his men rode out from St Donats Castle to meet them and captured Dolphyn and his men. They were hung the next day.

John Callice

The details of John Callice's birth and early life are not known, other than that he was born somewhere in South Wales in the early sixteenth century. As a young man he moved to London, joined the Royal Navy in 1571, and by 1574 was put in command of his first ship. It was in that year he seized an Italian merchant ship and sold off her cargo in Cardiff and Bristol, making a fortune. After that he plundered mercilessly, and he would frequently dispose of his cargos in South Wales, where he had developed a network of landowners and Royal officials, including the Vice-Admiral. He obviously had other friends in high places, because in May 1577, after he had been arrested and charged with six major cases of piracy, Queen Elizabeth I herself pardoned him at the request of the King of Scotland. As soon as he was released, he fled the country and headed to the Caribbean, where, for British naval officers, plundering Spanish ships was a way of life. He served under several privateer captains until taking command of his own ship, a captured French galleon. He eventually died in battle in the Mediterranean.

WILLIAM CHICK

William Chick was a big time pirate, operating extensively in the Bristol Channel. There is not a lot of information about him apart from one story. When he was captured, he was questioned (no doubt with some added encouragement from a thumb screw) and asked to give the names of his accomplices. He decided to turn informant and gave his guards the names of everyone he claimed was involved in piracy in Glamorgan. In doing so he revealed that most of the landed gentry in the county were on his payroll. Not surprisingly, no further action was taken against those he named, but he himself swung from the gallows.

THE SMUGGLERS OF BARRY ISLAND

Long before it became a beach resort and funfair, Barry Island was a real island. The causeway linking it to the mainland is a comparatively recent addition, and throughout this age of maritime lawlessness, it was the perfect smuggler's stronghold: a natural, sheltered harbour capable of holding a substantial ship (something put to good use during the industrial revolution); inaccessible for nine hours a day due to tides; and possessing plenty of coves in which to hide contraband.

It also would have been very remote, as the villages of Barry and Barry Island were at the time both little more than a cluster of cottages, far less significant even than other neighbouring villages like Cadoxton, Sully, Porthkerry or Penmark, and far away from the prying eyes of the authorities.

The earliest recorded account of Barry Island being used as a smuggler's base is from 1782, when excise men reported sighting a large cutter with twenty-four guns and a crew of forty moored off the island, openly running contraband goods. To put that into some context, the entire population of Barry at the time would not have been much more than forty people; in other words, pretty much everybody in the village was involved in this racket. For continuity, it is worth pointing out that Barry's parish church at the time was none other than the tiny little church at St Curig's, Porthkerry, which we discussed in our last chapter. If members of its congregation were smugglers during the week, it is perhaps hardly surprising that on a Sunday they might be heretics. I guess that the population of eighteenth-century Barry had something of a problem with authority.

The ship was likely to have belonged to a pirate and smuggler by the name of Thomas Knight, who came to Barry from Lundy. Within a year of arriving, he had begun to implement a grand vision for Barry Island. He didn't just want to smuggle the odd brandy barrel or bale of wool; he wanted to smuggle on an industrial scale. He quickly found that the willingness of the locals to get their hands dirty might be his greatest asset. He was very well organised and even went to the trouble of building some fortifications around the shoreline of the island, so he could control who came and went and, if need be, repel any unwanted attention from law enforcers or customs men.

It was reported by the local customs officer, a Thomas Hopkins of Sully, that Knight had a fighting force of between sixty to seventy men to defend the island. This may well have been an exaggeration, an attempt to get his local smuggling problem prioritised. Hopkins had terrible difficulty recruiting enforcers in the area, with the rebellious locals seeming to have far more respect for Knight than for the customs officers of the Crown. Exaggerated or not, the fortifications, fully crewed twenty-four gun ship, and a fighting force of any size clearly suggest that Thomas Knight was setting up a serious operation.

Once he was established, Knight ran an entire fleet of heavily armed ships to and from the Channel Islands, where he had contacts receiving consignments of contraband spirits and tobacco from pirates and smugglers off the coasts of France. He also sent ships to Ireland to return with contraband soap, another product that carried heavy excise duties at that time.

THE ROLE OF THE LOCAL PUBS IN BRIDGEND AND THE VALE

Thomas Knight's smuggling operation soon started to become a victim of its own success. Barry Island's remoteness, which had made it such an attractive place to set up shop, was now proving to be its biggest draw back. Goods needed to be transported over large distances to find their customers, and the poor roads compounded this. The only good roads of the time were the turnpikes, but these were not only toll roads but routinely patrolled by law enforcement; most significantly, the closest turnpike was in Wenvoe, and there were none in Barry or Barry Island. Not to mention, as we explored in the chapter about Cap Coch, road travel in the eighteenth century could be quite a dangerous undertaking.

With distribution so slow, cargos soon started to pile up on the island. Running out of places to hide contraband presented a big risk. What if the authorities got their act together and raided the island?

As I have said earlier, Thomas Knight was a very astute businessman who liked to think big. For someone with his commercial acumen, the solution was simple. He recruited smaller gangs of smugglers from further along the coast to act as his 'runners', turning his operation on Barry Island into one of a contraband wholesaler. The runners would row out to Barry Island, from their respective locations, and Knight would unload from his fleet of larger ships. The runners would buy for a reduced price as much contraband as they could fit into their little boats, then row back to their distribution depots and sell on to their own customers. Any surplus stock would have been hidden away somewhere secret but close by. One favourite hiding place was the cave at Witches Point, between Southerndown and Ogmore-by-Sea. This was perfect for clandestine use, only accessible at high tide and by boat.

Not being as well organised or financed as Knight, these runners did not have fortified hide outs with standing guards, but they all needed some kind of base from which to operate. This trade became the lifeblood of the old pubs and inns of the Heritage Coast. As we learned from the story of Cap Coch, pub landlords in this area were a pretty lawless bunch, and there is good reason to believe that many moonlighted as the kingpins of these runner gangs, or at least facilitated their activities through cooperation.

One of the main players was the landlord of the Captain's Wife in Sully. His gang unloaded their cargo in the harbour of Sully Island, and contraband was stored in the cellar of the pub, with any surplus hidden away in pits and caves on the island. Similarly, down the coast at Aberthaw (which at the time was a port on the river Thaw) a gang of runners operated from the Blue Anchor. They would have barrels unloaded on the port jetty in the dead of night and then roll them uphill to the pub for safe keeping. The barrels would have been wrapped in wool to dampen the noise they made and reduce the risk of their being punctured by rocks or debris on the ground.

Both the Sully and Aberthaw smugglers had to be especially vigilant, as there were customs officers stationed at both of these locations. However, this in reality might not have been quite the threat it first appears. In 1733 William Roberts, customs officer for Aberthaw, was instructed to raid Sully Island but refused; the last time he had done so, he had confiscated six barrels of brandy only to have his warehouse broken into and the brandy taken back in no short order.

Further down the coast, in Monknash, a similar operation was run from the Plough and Harrow and at the Portobello (now a private house) on the River Ogmore, near where it merges with the River Ewenny. This latter inn had its own jetty on the east bank, for boats to unload onto.

Knight's runners even carried booty as far west as Newton, Porthcawl (over twenty-seven miles from Barry Island), in a small rowing boat. The centre for distribution there was a pub that was then called the Ancient Mariner and is now the Jolly Sailor.

Activities in Llantwit Major centred around the Old Swan Inn. This pub stands out from the others, as at some point Knight made it his own headquarters, using it as a mainland base to organise this network of runners. Perhaps the landlord of the Old Swan was a favourite of his, or conversely, perhaps he had displeased Knight and lost his franchise, his pub, and very likely his life. Sadly, it is not clear.

The Old Swan Inn, Llantwit Major. From here Thomas Knight ran a network of smugglers and runners covering most of the South Wales coastline.

The authorities caught up with Thomas Knight in 1785, when the local customs officers joined forces and managed to muster enough enforcers to take on the standing guard on Barry Island and mount a raid. They confiscated what they could find, but Knight evaded capture as at the time he and his ships were sailing for Ireland. He took refuge on his home island of Lundy.

He is not known to have returned to Barry, but by this point he would have amassed a pretty substantial fortune. It seems likely that such a calculating figure would have had an exit strategy, and hidden away riches that he would be able to access if Barry Island ever fell. Not surprisingly, therefore, after this we never hear of him again.

THE SMUGGLER WILLIAM ARTHUR

The collapse of Thomas Knight's operations on Barry Island were a hollow victory for the law enforcers. It created a vacuum in the area, and soon someone who had been watching Knight's smuggling empire with interest moved in and took it over. This was a smuggler originally from Devon called William Arthur (who became known as the Smuggler King). He already ran a very successful operation from Gower, where he was reputed to have a gang of over 100 men; he also ran smuggling operations across the south west Wales coast. Being a hands-on sort of person, he is known to have visited all of his interests on a regular basis, to make sure everything was running as it should and to keep discipline amongst his crews. Woe betide anyone pilfering brandy for themselves. Like Knight, Arthur was known to be a brutal man if you crossed him.

For the authorities, he proved just as tough a nut to crack as his predecessor. Learning from the raid that had ousted

Thomas Knight, William Arthur reinforced his position on Barry Island still further. The local customs officer wrote to his superiors, describing the severity of the situation and declaring that it would take the effort of sixty dragoons to take the island and make it safe. As I said earlier, he was possibly prone to exaggeration.

However, the reinforcements came, and once again the customs men marched onto the island and overpowered those defending it, seizing nearly 300 casks of brandy and three chests of tea. William Arthur was not on Barry Island at the time, but he got his comeuppance on 13th April 1804, when customs officers raided his farm near Oxwich, Gower, seizing 420 casks of contraband spirits (about 3,000 gallons).

The last known use of Barry Island as a smugglers' den was in 1791. Symbolic of the dwindling fortunes of smugglers all around Welsh coasts, the crew's single ship, *the John O' Combe*, may have originally been a part of Thomas Knight's fleet of pirate ships.

CARADOG, TRIBAL KING OF THE SILURES AND HIS LEGACY

Caradog was a great Welsh tribal chief. Before the Romans came to Wales in the first century, he had fought and defeated his neighbours as far east as the Severn Estuary, making himself overlord of all the tribes in south east Wales. In doing so, he may well have made himself South Wales' first king (although this is a very contentious claim). What is commonly accepted, however, is that he was deeply respected by both his subjects and his enemies alike. For example, Dio Cassius, a great statesman and scholar of Rome, gave him the Latin name of Caractacus as a mark of respect.

Some legends have Caradog as living in or near Caerwent in Monmouthshire, but others say he lived at the hillfort at Dunraven in the Vale of Glamorgan. He and his armies managed to hold off the Roman invasion for over a decade, predominantly through a very successful campaign of guerrilla warfare. However, in full set-piece battle with the disciplined legions of Emperor Claudius, he was hopelessly outclassed. His forces were eventually defeated somewhere between Brecon and Cardiff. He fled to a kingdom known as Bigantes, in modern day northern England, but was betrayed by Queen Cartimandua, who ruled Brigantes, and handed over to the Roman authorities.

Known to the Romans as 'Caracticus – king of the Silures', Caradog was so greatly respected by his enemy that, after his defeat, his statue was erected in Rome itself.

Once captured he was deported to Rome, where he was sentenced to death by Emperor Claudius, but he is said to have given such a beautiful speech, full of fire, passion and emotion, that the emperor changed his mind and spared his life.

It was Rome that described him as the chief of the Silures, but in reality it is unlikely that the warriors he led would have identified with a single tribe. They were, at best, loosely allied under his command, and the label of a single tribe of '*Silures*' or '*Essyllwg*' is likely to be a Roman invention of convenience.

Around such a magnificent and historically significant character as this, there is bound to be a rich vein of legend and myth, and the bards do not disappoint. It is widely believed that the mythical character Caradog ap Bran is based on this charismatic chieftain.

THE LEGENDS OF CARADOG (CARADOG AP BRAN, AKA CARADOC AP BRAN)

Caradog ap Bran first appears as a character in the second of the Four Branches of the Mabinogi. These stories were written in the twelfth century in a language described by historians as 'Middle Welsh' and were the first ever attempt at recording a compilation of bardic legends in writing, and possibly the oldest secular storybooks ever written in the UK.

The legend we are looking at here is not actually about Caradog, but he does play a crucial role in the plot (which is quite a convoluted affair in its entirety).

In the legend, Caradog's father is Bran the Blessed, king of all Britain. Bran is also the human child of Llyr, the ancient sea god. Not long after Bran has brokered a marriage between his sister Branwen and Matholwch (*pronounced 'Ma-thol-ooch'*), the king of Ireland, their relationship turns sour. Matholwych, still furious about an insult dealt to him by Branwen's half-brother, takes his anger out on his new bride. Mistreated and banished from the kingdom, Branwen tames a starling to carry a message of her plight home to her brothers.

As you might have guessed there is a weight of symbolism tied up in her choice of messenger. The late eighteenth-century antiquarian John Aubrey writes that in Wales starlings are called 'Adar y Drudwy', which he translates into Latin as '*Avis Druidum*' or 'birds of the druids'. This could mean one of three possibilities: that druids kept starlings as companions; that they used them in religious ceremonies; or that starlings were considered the spirits of the druids themselves. Either way, by choosing a starling, Branwen is entrusting her secret to the bird of the Welsh druids, and invoking some magical protection from a Welsh ally in Ireland.

Her message gets through and a huge force is raised. They put to sea in warships, ready to invade Ireland, free Branwen and punish Matholwch. While they are gone, they leave Caradog in charge as the defender of Britain.

Caradog's scheming and conniving uncle, Caswallawn fab Beli (*pronounced 'Cass-wal-an fab Bee-lie'*), decides that now is his best chance to usurp Bran's throne. Armed with a magic cloak of invisibility, he passes through the forces left at Caradog's disposal and kills them all one by one until only Caradog remains, the kingdom's last defender. Despite his young age, his inexperience of battle and his adversary's use of magic, Caradog fights valiantly and nearly confounds this attempt at stealing the throne. But tragedy strikes when Caswllawn subdues him, his courage wanes to a feeling of despair and bewilderment, and ultimately Caswallawn triumphs.

Caradog, Caradoc, or an adulteration thereof is not always a Welsh chieftain or warrior. He exists in Saxon, French, Breton and Norman mythology. He is also a knight in the tales of King Arthur and the Knights of the Round Table. He also pops up in another legend, in which, after a valiant fight, he is tragically killed in battle and his head cut off and buried in the Tower of London, with it foretold that, one day, when the nation is in peril, he will rise up and defend it once more. The popularity of these legends meant that Caradog became a very popular name in post-Roman Britain. He was honoured and remembered through the choice of names for many later kings and princes of Wales, right up until the fourteenth century.

LEGACIES OF CARADOG IN THE VALE

We owe a lot to Caradog and to the family he left behind. The lands and tribes he united formed the basis of the kingdom of Morgannwg and the blueprint of South Wales as a whole. Also, a lot of his military defences are still visible in our landscape today.

Many of these settlements, although no doubt renovated by his warriors, are in reality a lot older than the first century. For example, the Bulwarks in Porthkerry date back to 2000 BC. Nonetheless they remain a visible reminder of his main lines of defence and offence during the Roman invasion. You can still see their remains across the region. His coastal fortifications were at Dunraven, Wick, Nash Point, Llantwit Major, Porthkerry, and Sully Island, with inland defences at

Llanblethian, Llancarfan, Dinas Powys and Caerau.

Another possible legacy was the establishment of the region's first commercial port. Much of the following is contested, but it is at least worth consideration as a possibility. Caradog left a son, Ceri, known as Ceri ap Caid, king of the Essyllwg. Being the son of the great tribal leader, and also obedient to Rome, he was appointed as governor of an area roughly corresponding to what is now the Vale of Glamorgan by the new Roman authorities. At the time, the valley in which Porthkerry Park is now located was a port. It is not a massive leap to speculate that it might have originally been called 'Port Ceri'. It was a very prosperous commercial port in its day, able to berth 100 ships by the year 286.

WHAT HAPPENED TO THE OLDEST SEAT OF LEARNING IN BRITAIN?

Some of the street names in the oldest part of Llantwit Major, such as College Street and College Gardens are clues to the location of a seat of learning that was established around 900 years before the universities at Oxford and Cambridge. In fact, it was established 700 years before any other known educational institution anywhere in the UK. It was Britain's first ever school, and it used to stand under what is now the parish church of St Illtyd, the name of which commemorates the saint who played such a pivotal role in the history of this institution.

It was originally called Cor Tewdws which translates as 'University College of Theodosius', and it is believed to have been founded round about the year 395 AD, at the tail end of the Roman occupation of Britain. You might be forgiven for thinking that what I am describing was no more than a room with a monk at one end and a handful of students at the other. But at its height, the Cor had over 2,000 students enrolled, across 400 different houses. Alumni included princes, theologians, academics and men from the very top of ancient society in Britain. Names associated with the college, either as students or masters, included St David, the patron saint of Wales; St Patrick the patron saint of Ireland; the Welsh bard Taliesin, author of *the Books of Taliesin*; and the sixth century monk Gildas the Wise, who wrote *De Excidio et conquest Britanniae*, one the Britain's earliest history books, cataloguing the rise and rule of the Saxons in England.

There is a reason why the output of the Cor was pretty much exclusively ecclesiastical. The institution was named in honour of Theodosius, the Roman emperor who in the year 380 AD had declared that Nicaean Christianity was the only legitimate religion of the empire. The college was established as a means to facilitate the deployment of Christian doctrine in missions throughout Britain and the known world.

With the protection of the Pax Romana, the institution thrived, but when the Romans left around 410 AD, it frequently fell victim to attack from pillaging Saxon, Irish, Scot and Pict marauders. It is even suggested that St Patrick was kidnapped by Irish bandits while he was at the Cor. The most brutal raid came in 446 AD, and it resulted in the buildings being burned to the ground and all the masters associated with the college being murdered or taken as slaves.

The site of the college was then abandoned for roughly sixty years, until 508 AD, when according to the twelfth-century *Book of Llandaff*, the evangelist St Dubricius instructed St Illtyd (a prince of Breton origin) to go with his patronage to the site of the old Cor, to rebuild and re-establish it as an institution of Christian learning. It was from this point that the college entered its golden age, and it is this second iteration of the institution that is the best known. That is why the blue plaque at the church records the college's foundation as being the work of St Illtyd and the date of its investiture as 500 AD, with no reference to the earlier body. St Illtyd's success in his mission resulted in the town being named as Llan-Illtyd Fawr (the Church of Illtyd the Great).

All that remains of the Cor, the first university institution ever established in Britain, is the church building and a few scattered ruins around the perimeter of the church yard in Llantwit Major.

The Llancarfan-born mediaeval poet and historian Edward Williams (who went by his bardic name of *Iolo Morgannwg*) wrote about the Cor in the eighteenth century. He described the site as containing seven churches around seven enclosures, each with seven companies, with seven cells for each company. Each company was made up of a choir containing seven learned men. A bit of quick arithmetic will tell you that, if these figures are correct, the Cor housed between 2000 and 2400 people.

In its second incarnation the college continued to thrive for over 500 years. So what went wrong? How could such a strong and unique institution, with such a great history, just disappear without a trace?

First of all, throughout its history it continued to be vulnerable to frequent sackings, initially from the Irish and then later the Vikings. The latter are meant to have totally destroyed it for a second time in 987 AD. The most crushing blow, however, came at the hand of someone we are already familiar with from previous chapters: one Robert Fitzhamon, feudal baron of Gloucester and conqueror of the ancient kingdom of Morgannwg. When his forces invaded the area, they sacked the college and took its religious artefacts, relics and treasures and transferred them all to the abbey at Tewkesbury. The college was reinstated in 1111, but depleted of authority and without the huge patronage that it would once have had, it could only limp on, like a wounded animal, at a vastly reduced scale. Finally, it was fully closed down on the order of Henry VIII, as part of the dissolution of the monasteries circa 1540.

All that remains of it now are the church buildings in the centre of the town.

BLOODY ENCOUNTERS: BATTLES OF THE VALE

A quick scan of the history books would suggest that no pivotal battles were fought on the fields of Glamorgan. We were too far removed from big events and the people who shaped them. Having said that, there was no shortage of bloody conflict here, and even though pitched tactical battles were thin on the ground, we did have a couple we can be proud of.

THE MASSACRE AT ST BRIDES

The earliest example dates back to the great defender of Wales, Caradog. I have mentioned fleetingly in an earlier chapter that he is believed to have once occupied the Iron Age hillfort at Dunraven, above Southerndown Beach. The fuel for that belief is a legendary battle which is meant to have been fought somewhere in the area. It was an especially ferocious and bloody affair in which Caradog's forces supposedly butchered vast numbers of a Roman legion. It is one of those legends that seems over the centuries to have fallen out of the bards' favour, so we only have fragments of it left. It has, however, been supported by modern day archaeology. A lot of bones dating from that period have been uncovered in fields near St Brides, which suggest that this battle was a very real historical occurrence.

While Caradog was able to provide the Romans with a temporary reckoning in our area, conflicts with the Normans generally seemed to have passed us by. Fitzhamon's invasion fought furiously to secure control of Morgannwg, but all the really big stuff happened outside our area. Most of the local battles were smaller scale raids, skirmishes and sieges rather than battles: incidents like the sacking of Kenfig, the monasteries and the Cor in Llantwit Major. There were also many, many reprisals, uprisings and rebellions against the Norman occupation but, again, all too small in scale to be described as battles.

The controversy around Stalling Down

But jump forward 400 years, to a field outside Cowbridge, and all this changes rather dramatically. At this time, Owain Glyndwr was leading a rebellion of Welsh lords against the English King Henry VI, with the aim of creating an independent Wales. The English establishment were hellbent on maintaining their Welsh holdings, and their clash led to some seething battles. The scene of one, and of one of Owain's greatest victories, is reputed to have been Stalling Down, a large open area of common land between the town of Cowbridge to the west, the village of Aberthin to the south and the village of St Hilary to the north. These days, the common is very popular with picnickers and dog walkers, many no doubt oblivious to its tempestuous past.

But before going any further, let's get the cynics dealt with first. The principal historical authority we have for this battle is someone we have spoken of already: the same source as we have for the layout and the number of students enrolled at Cor Tewdws, Edward Williams (aka Iolo Morgannwg). He was a historian from Llanblethian, near Cowbridge, who cast himself very much in the role of bard, thereby giving himself free reign to romanticise and potentially exaggerate. That is why his writings are approached, by some, with caution. The cynics' case is bolstered by the fact that Sir Robert Rees Davies, a very prominent twentieth-century Welsh historian, and esteemed authority on Owain Glyndwr's revolt, makes no mention of the battle of Stalling Down.

Clearly, *Davies* was not convinced; however, I, for one, believe that the battle did take place here, and I believe it for the following reasons:

> There are several things that make Stalling Down a really good place for a battle. It may sound quite basic, but moving armies around is a really difficult thing to do. Especially moving them around in such a way that your archers, infantry and cavalry all arrive in the same place at roughly the same time, and do so with their supporting corps in tow. Even in twenty-first century conflicts, getting this right can be something of a difficulty, so you can imagine that, in the fifteenth century, it would have been a massive headache. Accordingly, a battlefield

with a Roman Antonine road running along its northern flank would have been pretty handy. Then there is the terrain: a large, comparatively open area, with great visibility, climbing gently towards the north, dropping off into a scarp to the south towards Aberthin. It is also far enough away from any large civilian settlements to minimise the impact on innocent civilians, while still close enough to get supplies, provisions and medical attention.

Even though Edward Williams might have been prone to a bit of exaggeration, it is a big leap from embellishing a few details here and there to making up a landmark battle. And furthermore, his account is not the only one we have. It's simply the earliest *written* account, coming a few hundred years after the event. In common tales of folklore, however, there are plenty of accounts that preceded it, and it is these stories which Williams captured.

We have archaeological evidence of an event that occurred in the area around this time, an event that resulted in a lot of bodies. In 1896 the church at Llanblethian (only three miles or so from Stalling Down) had its floor excavated in preparation for building works. Under the floor they found a stone staircase, clearly leading to a crypt that, as far as they could work out at the time, was not detailed in any of the church records. Inside they found the skeletons of over 300 men piled high without

> coffins. A plague pit maybe? On a closer examination of the records, they discovered a reference to a crypt which was described thus: 'the burial place of the Sweeting family before the war with Owen Glyndwr'.
>
> Place names also add credibility. Street names often give us a snapshot of the history of an area, and the highest point of Stalling Down is known locally as Bryn Owain (Owain's hill).

When you question why we do not have any contemporary written account of this battle, you have to take into account the oft quoted maxim 'history is written by the victors' – attributed to Winston Churchill but, in reality, much older. It should come as no surprise that the ruling English did not go out of their way to write up this humiliating loss, and the fact that it took place in a rural backwater would have made supressing accounts relatively easy. So we end up with this lacuna in the records. If you thought that spin and fake news were twenty-first century inventions, think again.

THE BATTLE OF STALLING DOWN

In 1403 Owain Glyndwr was in Carmarthen, where word reached him that the English knew of his presence and were amassing a huge army to march west across Glamorgan to annihilate him and his forces. He sent his army east to meet the English, and the place they met was near Cowbridge.

Glyndwr's army was led by several prominent Welsh lords,

Rhys Gethin and Cadwagan, lord of Glynn Rhondda. In some accounts, Glyndwr himself was there as well, to lead from the front. His forces are also supposed to have been supported by legions from the French army, who were happy to back anyone looking to undermine the king of England.

The battle lasted for eighteen hours, with 'blood fetlock deep' on the horses that survived the battle. At the end of it the English were soundly beaten and retreated along the Antonine road to Cardiff, hotly pursued by Glyndwr's forces. The English retreat was confounded still further by the most atrocious weather conditions, most likely leading to further losses, if references to thunderstorms and flooding near Monmouthshire are accurate.

The only reason I question the accuracy of this detail is because our source for the weather is a bardic legend, and virtually everything in bardic legends is shrouded in some way in ancient Celtic symbolism. Thunderstorms after a victory in battle are often a big tick in the Celtic box. In Welsh, as well as other pagan Celtic mythology, the god of thunder is the protector of paradise.

The Battle of St Fagans

The history of this one is much less controversial.

Believed to be the biggest battle ever fought on Welsh soil, the Battle of St Fagans was fought in the spring of 1648, near where the National Museum of Welsh Life stands today. This was a battle from the era of the English Civil War, in which ultimately the forces of parliament, led by Oliver Cromwell, fought and won against the king of England, Charles I, to create 'a commonwealth' or republic.

Unlike a lot of accounts in this book, this one comes with a sea of verified historical records that tell us exactly what happened down to the fine details. It also comes against the twisting backdrop of what became known as the Second English Civil War. Why the second? Because the first civil war was over by 1647, but tempers continued to simmer below the surface, ultimately flaring up due to disagreements about unpaid wages and who was allowed to maintain their forces. In the second instalment, to keep things complicated, a lot of generals and their forces switched sides, so armies that had previously been loyal to the king became rebel forces and vice-versa.

In March 1648 a number of Welsh lords refused to hand over their castles as they had been commanded to. These were Colonel Poyer, governor of Pembroke Castle, Sir Nicholas Kemopys of Chepstow Castle and Colonel Powell of Tenby Castle. To confound this situation still further, the former Parliamentarian commander in South Wales, Major General Laugharne, had decided to change sides and was now loyal to the king and in command of what was now the rebel army.

Faced with rebellion in Wales, Sir Thomas Fairfax (Parliamentarian) dispatched a detachment of around 3,000 well-disciplined professional troops and cavalry of the New Model Army under the command of Colonel Thomas Horton. By now Laugharne's rebel army consisted of around 500 cavalry and 7,500 infantry, most of whom were volunteers or 'club-men' armed with just clubs and billhooks. Laugharne's army began to march on Cardiff but Horton managed to get there first, taking the town before the Royalists could do so. He made camp to the west of the town, by the village of St Fagans, and waited for reinforcements. Those reinforcements were a further Parliamentary force under the command of none other than Lieutenant-General Oliver Cromwell himself.

Cromwell would have been familiar with the area, as he had spent a lot of time there as a boy. His mother was from what was then just a village called Whitchurch, now a suburb of Cardiff. He is rumoured to have stayed at a coaching inn halfway up the Tumble on the night after battle. This used to be called the Treharne Arms, but these days is an Indian restaurant called the Marigold.

Major-General Laugharne was desperate to defeat Horton before Cromwell's army arrived, so after a brief skirmish on the 4th May, he decided to launch a surprise attack on the 8th May.

The two armies were encamped on either bank of the stream known as the Nant Dowlais, a tributary of the River Ely further north. Shortly after 7am that morning, Laugharne sent 500 of his infantry to attack the Parliamentary outposts. The well-trained Parliamentarians easily repulsed the attacks. The battle then degenerated into guerrilla combat, with the Royalist troops hiding in and attacking from behind hedges and ditches where the Parliamentarian cavalry were less effective. Gradually however the training of the Parliamentarian troops and their superior number of cavalry told; Horton's army began to advance and the Royalists began to panic.

A last ditch attempt to rally the Royalist forces – a cavalry attack led by Laugharne himself – failed, and within just two hours, the Royalist army had been routed. 300 Royalist troops had been killed and over 3000 taken prisoner, the remainder fleeing west to Pembroke Castle with Laugharne and his senior officers. Here they endured an eight-week siege before surrendering to Cromwell's forces.

LLANTWIT MAJOR RIOTS

For such a sleepy little rural town, Llantwit Major has a past tainted by many incidents of lawlessness and violent, bloody murder. Not just in the eighteenth century when Thomas Knight held court over his cut-throat band of smugglers and pirates; 300 years earlier it was held in the grip of a gangland feud that one day erupted into rioting on the streets.

The families at the centre of it all were no strangers to violence. Seventy years before the main event, in 1527, one Thomas Vann of Marcross was found guilty of murdering John Fleming under the town hall at Llantwit Major. 'Under the town hall' may sound a bit odd, but the likely explanation is simple. In the sixteenth century, a new town hall had been built on the site of the old one, and this new building was split across two floors, with the lower floor used for shops and market stalls, and the upper floor by the church and clerks for administrative affairs (including court hearings). Accordingly, the murder must have happened on the lower floor of the new town hall building. This is the first recorded incident related to the Vann family, but it is certainly not the last.

The sleepy streets of Llantwit Major were a smouldering volcano, poised to erupt into violent rioting.

The second came on Sunday 9th October 1597. Two brothers, Edward and Edmund Vann, and a number of other accomplices burst into the church of St Illtyds in Llantwit Major during the Eucharist service, to attack members of the Seys family of Boverton in front of the priest and the entire congregation. One member of the Seys family was stabbed, and the Vanns and their gang are said to have spent the following hours rioting on the streets of Llantwit Major. The incident was reported as 'a ryott and other misdemeanours, with the use of daggers and throwing of stones causing utmost damage to the town and people'.

Several hours passed before the local justice of the peace was sent for. This was one Sir Edward Stradling of St Donats

Castle (who you may recall from a previous chapter for his writing of the legend of the twelve knights). Not a man to be trifled with, Sir Edward sent for a small detachment of soldiers, who escorted the Seys family home to safety under armed guard and then turned their attention to bringing the riotous Vanns to heel. The gang were captured and taken to London for trial.

On 28th August 1598, after a hearing at the court of the Star Chamber, Edmund, Edward and their accomplices were incarcerated in Fleet Prison to await their trial. Needless to say the brothers were found responsible for the incident, and by 9th February 1599, Edmund was fined £1,000 (enough to buy a house) with £100 to be paid to Roger Seys, whilst Edward was fined 500 marks.

Fortunately, Llantwit Major has calmed down a lot these days, and incidents of rioting have been cut right back to a minimum.

BANDITS FROM THE HILLS

There are some amazing panoramic vistas to be seen from the hills to the north of Bridgend and the Vale. Many of them were utilised by the ancient Britons, such as at Castell Kribor, an Iron Age hillfort which gave its name to the nearby village of Cefn Cribwr. From such a vantage point, the hill dwellers had a good view of exactly what was going on in the lowlands below. This afforded them great advantages in military matters, both in defence and attack, as it did too in later history for bandits and outlaws.

Taffy was a Welshman

It is widely known that many seemingly innocent children's nursery rhymes are in reality about some pretty grim subject matter. One of the best known examples is 'Ring a ring o' Rosies', which is actually about how London was ravaged by the Black Death – one of the darkest episodes in British history repackaged in a little ditty of childlike innocence.

Here is another nursery rhyme of this kind, one that any Welsh child who, like me, was educated in an English school will have heard a few times too many:

> 'Taffy was a Welshman
> Taffy was a thief,
> Taffy came to our house
> And stole a leg of beef.'

Where does this notion come from? Again, the answer is a morbid one. While there is a verifiable history of Welsh banditry in the Vale and Bridgend area, the motivations of the raiders, as is often the case, were rooted in privation, oppression and desperation.

When the Normans invaded Morgannwg, it was to places like Cefn, the Garw, Maesteg, Ogmore and the Rhondda valleys that the Welsh were confined. The poor soil in these upland areas was not capable of producing crops and barely even able to support the grazing of cattle. Meanwhile, the wealthy and well-defended Norman families kept and farmed the much more bounteous fields of the lowland areas around coastal parts of Bridgend and the Vale of Glamorgan. Initially the raids of the hill-bound Welsh were uprisings and rebellions attempting to retake their lands. More latterly however, they were launched for more practical reasons. They needed the food.

As captured by this contemporary account:

> 'in the lower mountains in the ffrontyers of the low country, with often rodes and incurtions, assayled the Strangers, sometimes out of one part of the

> mountains, sometimes out of another, and taking them at advantage often slew great companies of them… taking from them preys and booties, whereby they sustained themselves. For the mountains in those days bare noe such corne as now growth thereon.'

As you would expect, the Normans took these incursions very seriously, poaching of any kind punishable by death from a full day of torture. So the telling of the nursery rhyme should not have goaded me as much as it did as a child. In reality it's all about rock-hard Welsh tribesmen risking their lives to take back what was rightfully theirs, in order to feed their people. Something to feel quite proud of, really.

THE CEFN RIDERS AND THE RED GOBLINS

In 1780 an industrialist called John Bedford moved to the area from Birmingham, established a blast furnace and sunk several coal mines around Cefn, Aberkenfig and Kenfig Hill. In these early days of the industrial revolution, such an opportunity for work attracted large numbers of economic migrants from exotic and far flung places such as Neath and Cowbridge. But the boom was short lived. Bedford died only eleven years later, in 1791, and the trustees of his estate scaled back the operation massively as it was not making a sufficient profit. A lot of the families who had moved to the village suddenly lost their jobs, and in the absence of any form of welfare state, they had few options. Those who could moved on. Those who remained struggled to make a living any way they could.

This desperate situation created a hotbed of recruits for a band of cut-throats known as the Cefn Riders. From their vantage point in the village, they could see packmen making their way along the Antonine road, either climbing the hill from Margam to the west or on the opposing peak at Stormy Down to the south. They could see drovers moving their herds to Smithfield, and they could see when farms below them were gathering in their harvests.

Initially they acted as opportunistic highwaymen, operating on the Antonine road where it passed close by to the village, at the crossroads in Pyle. As time went on, however, they became more brazen and adventurous. They would set out on foot to rob with menace and assault all over South Wales, with incidents reported as far away as Merthyr Tydfil and Llantwit Major. They had a fearsome reputation for brutality and showed little mercy to their victims.

You may be wondering, if they would set out on foot, why were they known as 'the Cefn Riders'? It comes down to their modus operandi: they took sadistic pleasure in leaping onto the backs of travellers they robbed, forcing them to carry them a great distance until they were too exhausted to take another step and collapsed with exhaustion. It was a great way to make sure their victims did not give pursuit. The Welsh novelist Alexander Cordell borrowed from an account of one of their attacks in his book *The Fire People*.

We know slightly less about another pack of bandits from the area, known as the Red Goblins. We do know that they were semi-troglodyte, having their lairs in caves in the northernmost reaches of the Maesteg valley. And we know that they mounted raids across the Vale of Glamorgan. On one occasion they intercepted the Carmarthen drovers on their way to

Smithfield and relieved them of their entire herd. They were also not averse to a bit of kidnapping, and once captured a lady from the aristocratic Carne family of Llysworney, holding her for ransom. The Red Goblins did not have the same reputation for sadistic brutality as the Cefn Riders; in fact, their treatment of their aristocratic captive was described as 'honourable and courteous'. This has led some to level the accusation that the ranks of the Red Goblins were not just desperate law breakers, but also included some well-connected members who joined in for the exhilaration of it.

These tales about desperate bandits of the northern uplands litter history right up until the beginning of the nineteenth century. There is no doubt that when the Welsh were banished to the hills at the beginning of the twelfth century, Robert Fitzhamon set a social and economic blueprint which has continued down the ages. Technically, it could be argued that it still prevails right up to this day.

The hilly region in the northern quarter of Bridgend County (and in our neighbouring counties in South Wales) are more commonly referred to these days as 'the valleys'. There is a lot of poverty and social deprivation associated with these areas, although it is generally attributed to their recent industrial decline. The fact is that at no point in post-Norman history has it ever been particularly different. But it *was* different before this. There is a lot of archaeology which proves that before the Norman annexation, knights, nobles, princes and even kings lived in both upland and lowland areas in relatively equal measure, from Hirwaun to Blackmill and from Cefn Criwbr to the Garth. But not after.

Today's valley communities contrast very sharply with the

neighbouring leafy towns and villages of lowland areas, such as the Vale of Glamorgan and the coastal parts of Bridgend. These latter areas have long been where the wealthier tend to live, highlighted by the fact that the tiny market town of Cowbridge (which is no more than eight miles from the start of the valleys) can boast more resident millionaires than the rest of Wales added together.

We also have other hangovers from the annexation which are far more subtle and much harder to define but nonetheless, I believe, still hark back to this event. I remember my grandmother would always refer to any family from north of Bryncethin as being 'proper Welsh', even though she swore blind that she had nothing but Welsh blood coursing through her veins. Why the distinction? What made them more 'proper' than her? Another example: when I was a student, I used to work behind a bar in a well-known Cardiff pub called the Beverly. I frequently remember some of the clientele in casual conversation referring to people from the Valleys as 'the Welsh'.

As unlikely a source as it might be, the folk singer Frank Hennessey sums up what I am describing here in a folk song called 'Citizen of Cardiff'. The song itself is a tongue in cheek anthem of the attitudes of a typical Cardiffian of the 1970s, at a time when the signs in Cardiff were all having Welsh translations added. There is a verse which wrestles with the question of why it is that people in Cardiff feel like they are a different type of Welsh to the people who live in the hills and valleys to the north. In it, the singer argues that since the industrial revolution, Cardiff has always been full of diverse ethnic communities from all over the world and Cardiffians get along fine with all of them, just not with the 'Welsh'. Yet the verse goes on:

'Oh but I'm as Welsh as any other Taffy,
I shouts for homsey down at the Arms Park,
I can hum "Land of my Father's" with the next man,
And I even knows two lines of Sospan Fach…'

I realise that what we are cataloguing here are colloquialisms and feelings that are to some extent indescribable and subjective. But I am certain that the general sentiment, which will be recognisable to any local with roots in the area, originate from this annexation from over 900 years ago.

PART TWO

HALF-TRUTHS, MYTHS AND THE SUPERNATURAL

EARLY CHRISTIAN LEGENDS AND MIRACLES

Christianity first came to this part of Wales with the Romans in the latter part of the fourth century. Early churches and religious institutions like the Clas at Llancarfan and the Cor at Llantwit Major were founded in the 100 years that followed, spearheading its spread. Out of these establishments came a long succession of saints, either as students or masters, including St Cadoc (who is credited with establishing the Clas), St Illtyd (who established the second Cor), St Patrick, St David and St Cupricious. The canonisation of a saint in the ancient Catholic church required proof that the person in question 'either in life, or in death, had either directly or in answer to prayer' performed miracles. Such a cast of saints must mean a fair few miracles were witnessed in and around the Vale. And some, as you might expect, were truly weird.

As we go through these stories, it is interesting to note that early Christian legends are still rammed full of pagan Celtic symbolism. The Welsh in our area were keen to lap up the new religion but also to keep the old one running alongside it – a trend that we can still see much later in history, as we explored in our chapter about the Marian Cult in Porthkerry. It's like wanting to keep a spare just in case.

ST CADOC AT LLANCARFAN

We know quite a bit about this ancient Welsh saint, thanks to a biography called *Vitae Cadoci* that was written about him in the late eleventh century by a local man called Lifris of Llancarfan. St Cadoc had a rather colourful life. He was most likely to have been born in Monmouthshire and lived from 497 to 580. He was born a prince in a Welsh royal family, his kingly father a man predisposed to violence and raiding who had made a lot of enemies. His uncle was St Petroc, who went on to become the patron saint of Cornwall, himself a key figure in establishing monasteries in Padstow and Bodmin.

Cadoc was a real dab hand at miracles, to the extent that he is credited with performing some whilst still in the womb. One such miracle saw the cellars of his parents' house miraculously filled with food. Also, a holy well is said to have sprouted from the water he was baptised in, which thereafter frequently ran with wine or milk.

The legend of how he came to choose Llancarfan as the seat for his great monastery is equally bizarre. Supposedly, one day Cadoc was walking in woods in Glamorgan when a shepherd from an enemy tribe recognised him and launched at him with a weapon. Cadoc was unarmed (and not a fighting man) so he turned and ran away into the woods, right into the path of an angry wild boar, white with age. The wild boar was as furious as the shepherd, and charged at Cadoc. But before impact, it just vanished, as did the shepherd. Realising that he had been spared by God for a purpose, Cadoc marked the spot where this miracle had occurred with two sticks, and this was where he chose as the site for the monastery at Llancarfan. While building the Clas (as it became known), labouring monks reported that two stags came from the woods and helped with the carrying of timbers and building materials. From then, the stream that runs through Llancarfan has been known as Nant Carfan (Stag Brook), while Llancarfan itself translates as 'the church of stags'.

Looking for some subliminal Celtic symbolism? In many old stories the wild boar is a symbol of tenacity. There is an ancient tale from *the Mabinogion* where a prince called Culhwch (pronounced Kul-ooch) is set a number of tasks by a giant called Ysbaddaden (pronounced Uss-ba-tha-den), which he must complete if he is to win the hand of the giant's beautiful daughter Olwen. One of the tasks is to trim the giant's beard, and the only thing sharp enough is the tusk of a wild boar. Another task is to cut the giant's hair, and the only scissors up to the job belong to an Irish king who is able to transform himself into a wild boar with poisonous tusks.

Stags are massively important in Welsh Celtic folklore. They have several meanings: firstly, they are the kings and princes of the forest, their antlers serving as crowns. They also appear to carry the forest on their backs. Accordingly, a stag as a labouring prince carrying a heavy burden can be seen as a metaphor for Cadoc's mission to establish a church for God.

Having said that, it is worth noting that, in portraits of Cadoc's saintly uncle, St Petroc, he is usually pictured in the company of a wolf and a stag. It could be that the Celtic Cornish used the stag to symbolise the same meanings as the Celtic Welsh with Cadoc. Another possible explanation, given the family connection between these two, is that the stag was the tribal standard their ancestors followed into battle (in the same way that Roman legionaries marched into battle behind the standard of the eagle).

Stags in Celtic folklore are also associated with great sexual prowess (which is what a stag night is all about – preparing a groom for the consecration of a marital bed) but that's probably not so relevant in this instance. I just thought I would throw it in.

Fifteenth-century murals depicting sinners being consumed by a beast, on the walls of St Cadoc's church, Llancarfan, which is built on the site of the monastery established by the saint himself in the fifth century.

WHEN CADOC MET ILLTYD

There is another great legend about St Cadoc, concerning how he first met the man who was to become his most accomplished student and founder of the Cor in Llantwit Major – none other than St Illtyd.

Illtyd also had royal heritage, but his path to sainthood was quite different from Cadoc's. Cadoc's father had always wanted his son to be a warrior, but Cadoc had disappointed him by dedicating himself to the church. Conversely, Illtyd's family (who were Breton royalty) wanted him to go into the church, but instead he took a wife and committed to a military career, becoming a warrior knight. No doubt he wanted to follow in the footsteps of his cousin, the legendary King Arthur of Round Table fame.

One day, Illtyd was leading a hunting party and ventured onto lands belonging to Llancarfan. He sent word to Cadoc demanding hospitality. Cadoc found the unsolicited request from someone he did not know rather rude, but he agreed to it and the hunting party arrived at Llancarfan. Before anyone could eat anything, however, the ground opened and swallowed them up as punishment for their impertinence. Only Illtyd himself survived, and he dropped to his knees before Cadoc, begging forgiveness. Cadoc told him that the only path to absolution was to dedicate his life to God. Realising the wise abbot was right, Illtyd gave up his life of battle and war and became a hermit, only emerging when he believed himself to be pure and absolved of his sins, able to champion the scriptures. Which all seems a bit harsh – all he did was invite himself to dinner!

In the Catholic church St Cadoc is to this day the patron saint of victims of famine, deafness and glandular disorders.

His feast day is 25th September. He was killed, or rather martyred, defending religious relics from a raiding party of Saxon warriors.

ST DUNWYD AND THE PHANTOM SHIP

I promised you a weird miracle and this one will not disappoint. It is not clear when it is meant to have happened, whether it was during the life of its central figure, St Dunwyd, or much later, when he was a spirit. It was quite commonly told in the nineteenth century by sailors from Porthcawl.

St Dunwyd was a fifth-century Welsh Bishop and friend of St Cadoc. His name became anglicised to 'St Donats' in later history and was given to the castle and village where the Atlantic College now sits, near Llantwit Major.

The legend has it that at some point the nearby coastline was frequented by a three-masted barque which had sailed from the underworld. It sailed up and down the coast, spreading the pungent smell of sulphur, a stench so strong it was too much for the coastal inhabitants to live with. In this ship, the devil himself had placed the souls of sinners. On the shore one day, St Dunwyd spotted the devil counting the number of souls on board, so he threw a spear that punctured the hull and sank the ship. The devil had to swim for his life and all the souls on board were lost to him. He was fuming. The remains of the ship were spotted by a giant who lived on Gower, who reached down and made toothpicks out of the masts and handkerchiefs out of the sails – an early and important example of recycling to keep our seas and beaches clean!

THE MIRACLE OF THE CROSS IN ST DONATS & THE SCANDAL OF SIR THOMAS STRADLING

Sir Thomas Stradling was the father of Sir Edward Stradling, who we spoke about in our chapter on the legend of the twelve knights. The Stradlings were a noble family who lived in St Donats Castle and owned an estate that ran as far west as Merthyr Mawr and as far east as Boverton.

There is a small village on the estate near St Donats, called Marcross. It was named after a miraculous apparition of Christ on the cross manifested itself in full view of a traveller on the road to Wick. When the apparition subsided, he took some sceptical locals to the scene only to find that the apparition had burned an impression onto a tree that was as clear as day for all to see. Those assembled fell to their knees and rejoiced.

The story I am about to tell is also connected with the St Donats estate, and with crosses and trees, but it had rather more serious consequences. This account is lifted straight from contemporary reporting.

In woods on the estate, a cross was discovered in the hollow of a tree that had been blown down in a gale. It was quite a large cross, described as 'the size of a man's foot'. There is no mention made of what the cross was made out of.

Stradling believed that this discovery was miraculous and took the cross to London to display it for all to see. He also had copies of it made, which he began selling as relics. This was brought to the attention of Queen Elizabeth I herself, and she was not best pleased. Stradling was arrested and taken to the Tower, but throughout his incarceration he maintained his innocence and that the cross was a legitimate miracle. A commissioner was sent to examine the tree and brought bits of it back to London, but nothing miraculous was found. Despite his protestation, Sir Thomas realised that he was in serious trouble and was quick to apologise. As his representative pleaded:

> 'for yf he had knowen or thought that yo'r Highnes or you'r Counsell wolde have been offended there with or takenin yll harte, he wolde not for anything have done it'.

It had the desired effect. Sir Thomas was eventually released and fined 1000 marks 'to punish massmongers for the rebating of their humours'. He is reputed to have been kept under close surveillance by Elizabeth's agents for the rest of his life. No wonder his son was keen to find a story to elevate his family's social status.

If you are looking for plausible explanations for this story beyond 'miracle', then the chances are that, if the cross contained precious stones or metals, it was hidden in the tree by a monk from nearby Llantwit Major's Cor. If a warning came of approaching marauder ships, whether of Viking, Pict or Irish origin, then valuable treasures would have been spread out and hidden to confound those who would steal them. If the person who hid it was then slaughtered in the raid, then it would have remained hidden, its location a secret until the storm revealed it. Another possibility is that it was already stolen, and then hidden for safekeeping, but the thief died before being able to retrieve it.

*

THE GOBLIN STONE

In the grounds of Merthyr Mawr House there are the remains of a chapel believed to have been built on the site of a much older Celtic place of worship. Several old stone crosses have been found there. One, the Goblin Stone, had magical powers. The legend goes that it emanated a force that drew in passers-by and compelled them to embrace it. Once in an embrace, their hands and feet became entangled in the intricate carvings, forcing them into a position of 'prayer'. (To be fair, I think this experience would be enough to make anyone pray, no force required.)

Stones feature a lot in mythology (after all, King Arthur pulled his sword out of one). The legend that seems most related to this story is that of the Adder Stones (or in Welsh, *Glain Naidir*). Adder Stones appear a lot in many different Celtic traditions. They are glassy in appearance, with a hole in the middle supposedly created by burrowing snakes during the performance of a druidical ritual. In Welsh mythology they endow the holder with invisibility or allow them to fight an invisible foe. In our legend, something invisible is forcing people to kneel and pray. Possibly a bit tenuous, I accept, but the closest antecedent I can find.

THE LEGENDS OF ST JOHN'S WELL

You can still visit St John's Well, also known as Sandford's Well, on the green in the old bit of Newton, Porthcawl. It is opposite the twelfth-century church of St John on Beach Road.

From the outside it looks fairly innocuous. It has a stone wall built around it, no doubt from some point in history when controlling who was allowed to draw water became a priority. In the twentieth century, barbed wire and other metal defences were added to the wall to keep vandals out. The end result is that most people do not even know it's there. Recently I was telling someone the history and story of the well, and they confessed that they had always thought that the wall was some kind of secure lock up for gardening equipment, not a twelfth-century holy shrine.

The well was established when a knight called Sir Thomas De Sandford returned from the Crusades. He was a knight of the order of St John, which has a fascinating history all of its own. They, like the better known Templar Knights, were a warrior band of holy men. Having been sent to fight in the

Crusades, they were left behind in the region to guard Jerusalem from future attack. They set up headquarters on Cyprus and Rhodes and, after being chased out by the Ottoman Turks, were gifted the island of Malta by the Pope, where their mark is still felt to this day. The St John's order was known as Knights Hospitaller, which means that they founded hospitals and tended to the wounded on the field of battle – a tradition maintained to this day by the St John's Ambulance service.

You may recall in the legend of the lost city of Kenfig that a peasant boy is said to have visited an old knight who had fought in ancient battles before committing his later years to God. There is a possibility that this was a reference to Sir Thomas De Sandford. The fact that, by the time Kenfig was supposedly engulfed by water, De Sandford would have been over 300 years old does not necessarily rule him out. Once bards found a good character, they would often re-use them, sometimes even changing their names so as not to break the continuity of the rest of the story (see the later chapters on Maids of Cefn Ydfa and Sker for examples of this).

De Sandford fits the bill for several reasons: he was a local knight, and as we are about to discover, he had another water-related legend accredited to him. Also, his association with St John, who was said to have been present at the baptism of Christ, chimes nicely with the idea of his ghost employing water to purge Kenfig of sin.

Thomas De Sandford returned to Britain after fighting alongside members of Robert Fitzhamon's family and possibly alongside the great man himself. De Sandford was well rewarded for his loyalty. After his conquest of Morgannwg, Fitzhamon gifted land around Porthcawl to Sandford as a dowry. That is why both the well and the church at Newton are dedicated to St John. Though whether De Sandford himself ever actually spent any time there is unclear. He also had estates in Shropshire, which is where he made his home.

The miraculous well of St John in Newton, Porthcawl, is shrouded in legend and folklore.

During the Middle Ages, the waters of the well were said to have incredible healing powers. Numerous miracles were reported: people with life-changing injuries were healed and the lame made able to walk. No doubt all of these stories were related to the Hospitaller traditions of the order of St John.

But the well had another peculiarity. When the tide at the nearby beach is fully in, the well is always empty, but when the tide is out, the well is always full. This phenomenon had everyone perplexed. Even R.D. Blackmore himself was intrigued, writing:

> 'It comes and goes, in manner, against the coming and going of the sea, which is only half a mile from it: and twice a day it is many feet deep, and again, not as many inches. And the water is so crystal clear, that down in the dark it is like a dream… The children are all a little afraid of it… partly because of its maker's name… and partly on account of its curious ways, and the sand coming out of its nostrils when first it begins to flow'.

Such a phenomenon has attracted tales, legends and superstition in abundance. People used to go to the well to scourge themselves with whips or tree branches to atone for their sins, as it was seen as a conduit to the saints. It was also believed that if you were to take water from the well and bottle it, then it would remain pure, clean and fresh for a whole year. If you were to collect water from the well but then spill some, this was an omen of bad luck. Also, if two people wanted to wash at the well at the same time, they had to make the sign of the cross before proceeding. And there is a patch of sand on the beach at Newton where sand is said to 'dance' for no discernible reason, a phenomenon which can be freely observed to this day. The area where this happens is known as St John's Spa.

However, the most colourful story is about a holy man who was drawing water from the well when he spotted three frogs watching him. The largest frog was in fact the devil sent to tempt him, but fortunately for the holy man, the other two frogs turned out to be angels in disguise, who waited until Satan had revealed his intentions before attacking him and seeing him off.

A story about two frogs joining forces to attack a bigger one, with some seriously speculative interpretation added on by the spade load… It is tempting to speculate that this legend may have been fuelled by the accidental eating of *psilocybin* (also known as magic mushrooms), which used to flourish on the warm and damp, south-facing sand marshes around Porthcawl.

There is of course a perfectly rational, scientific explanation for the anti-tidal nature of the well. I am not a scientist, but I can summarise that is down to a freak geological occurrence where the movement of the tide creates pressures on plates running along the spring source of the well. This causes it to fill and empty in reverse countenance with the moving tides. There is a much more thorough explanation on the website of the parish church of St John, Newton, the modern-day custodians of the well.

WHEN THE DEVIL APPEARED ON CRACK HILL

In the early days of Christianity in Wales, the bards were understandably reluctant to give up all the colourful Celtic tales they had been telling for generations, even though a lot of them were based on paganism. To satisfy everyone, the bards would continue to tell these much older legends, replacing any monsters or grisly creatures either with the devil or, more commonly, the devil disguised as a beast. This means that in Wales we have a lot of stories about the devil and evading his evil clutches, but not so many about doing good deeds or following Christ and his saints.

An example is the once widely held belief that if a fire was slow in taking light, then the devil was sitting on the chimney and everyone in the house had to guard against mischief. This is directly lifted from an ancient Celtic legend about a forest sprite who fell in love with a woodcutter and would sit on his chimney. This would make his house fill with smoke so he would have to step outside until it cleared, giving her a chance to gaze upon him.

In time this inordinate focus on the devil would create a dread of sin in Welsh Christian culture, which in turn helped the 'clean living' non-conformist chapels get a strong grip on the country. While none of the stories that follow are bardic Welsh legends, they demonstrate the abiding hold of their devil-centric mythmaking on the Welsh imagination.

The following two episodes were told by two unrelated travellers under oath. At the time, these stories were widely believed to be true, because, though both episodes happened towards the end of the nineteenth century, they occurred at different times and neither of the men concerned had ever had any dealing with the other.

The first account comes from a man who had been travelling from Bridgend to Cowbridge late at night. His journey as far as the base of Crack Hill had passed without incident, but as he began his ascent of the steep hill, he found his footsteps becoming unaccountably slow. He struggled on, finding it harder and harder to keep up any pace. He then became aware of a sensation as if he were carrying a heavy weight. He looked sideways and found that something or someone had jumped on his back and was riding him in a way best described as a piggyback.

In a blind panic he tried to break into a run but found the weight of his passenger was forcing him to his knees. He tried to shake it off but could not. Gritting his teeth, his breath coming painfully in short bursts, he lumbered on. Near the top of the hill he was so exhausted he found himself sinking to the ground in despair, at which point he cried out to God for help. Immediately the weight left his back and he saw the shape lying on the roadway in a bundle.

Then, before his astonished eyes, it began rolling back down the hill. As it rolled it picked up speed, until it was careering towards the base. At the bottom of the hill it bounced into a disused quarry and exploded into a shower of sparks and smoke. The man is said to have run the rest of the way to Cowbridge, hardly daring to draw a breath.

The second incident, like the first, concerned a man traveling from Bridgend to Cowbridge at night, on this occasion on a horse and trap. Again, nothing out of the ordinary happened on the trip as far as the base of Crack Hill, but halfway up the slope, the horse began to slow its pace until it was barely moving at all.

Several times the trap lurched as the animal stumbled, and the man was sure he could make out a dark shape which must have been adding a huge weight to the shaft of the trap. He also felt a presence that he could not explain or describe, other than it filled him with fear and made him feel sick to his stomach. Near the top of the hill the horse came to a full stop, behaving as if startled by something. Panic-stricken, its eyes glaring red with fear, it stood rooted to the ground. The man called out to God for salvation, and immediately the strange object fell from the trap's shaft, twisted around on itself and went shooting down the hill. At the bottom, once again, it too bounded into the quarry and exploded into a mass of flame and smoke, and the air was thick with the smell of sulphur.

This is a very interesting reference. Sulphur is a naturally enough occurring element for ordinary people to have been familiar with it in the nineteenth century, either by the chemical name or its ancient name, brimstone. The smell of sulphur (which you are most likely to encounter in mould or rotten eggs) has long been associated with unfriendly spirits and demons. In the Bible, God destroys the cities of Sodom and Gomorrah with a rain of fire and brimstone (Genesis 19-21) and in Revelations 19 we are told that the Devil will be thrown 'into the lake of fire that burns with brimstone' meaning 'the second death' or complete annihilation.

Suffice it to say, the connection was not lost on the God-fearing folk of the area, and night-time trips up Crack Hill were strongly discouraged for quite a long time after.

There seem to be a disproportionately high number of traditional Welsh legends about the Devil, and he was reported to have appeared to terrified travellers between Bridgend and Cowbridge in the nineteenth century.

These were not the only times 'old nick' was reported in our area. Again in the nineteenth century, in the back room of a pub near the colliery in Maesteg, a group of coal miners reported a stranger had walked in and asked if he could join their game of cards. They obliged and dealt him in. After a short period of seeming normality, the mysterious gambler started to win on nearly every hand. He had all but cleared them out when he decided to celebrate his good fortune by leaping onto a table and dancing. Immediately, the eagle-eyed miners spotted that he had cloven hooves for feet, and they all ran screaming for cover. When the landlady (who was made of sterner stuff) went into the room to check on their claims, the stranger had vanished.

People in South Wales had a strange way of dealing with mentions of the devil. If he ever cropped up in a church reading, at the mention of his name the entire congregation would repeatedly spit on the floor to show their contempt – a practice that only died out in the nineteenth century, when spitting was banned in public to contain the spread of tuberculosis.

THE GIFTING OF SOUTHERNDOWN COMMON

We have spoken at length about the Norman invasion of Morgannwg, which yielded so many great stories and legends. On a few of those occasions, it has also been mentioned that the Welsh did not respond well to subjugation. Uprising and insurrection were the names of the day, as the Welsh refused to accept the confiscation of their land and the loss of their rights to hunt wherever they pleased. As we have already discussed, it was a time of desperation and poverty. But one incident from this era gave rise to a lovely story.

The castle and estate of Ogmore were given to the De Londres family by Fitzhamon. William De Londres was himself one of the fabled twelve knights and had a fierce reputation for coming down heavily on Welsh disobedience – a tendency put to the test on the day covered in this particular legend.

His son, Maurice De Londres, was hunting in the woods

around his family's castle when he caught a local Welshman poaching – a man who turned out to be of princely descent who had just let fly an arrow at a deer. He was immediately captured, beaten and taken to the castle to be hurled into a dungeon. The punishment for poaching was very severe: a day of torture, usually conducted in the forecourt of the castle as a spectacle for the family and their guests.

The next morning the instruments of torture were being heated up in preparation, and the prisoner was brought out into the yard for the first part of the torture, which was for him to be blinded.

The noble captive, however, stood stoic and proud with an air of unrepentant arrogance in the morning sun. His demeanour impressed everyone, especially the daughter of Lord Ogmore, who began to plead his case. She reminded her father that it was they, the Normans, who had taken everything away from the Welsh, and as it was her birthday, she wished that this man's life might be spared. De Londres, who was clearly in a good mood that day, obliged. So, taking advantage of his good humour, she decided to push further. She begged that the Welsh be given a reserve of land on which they could hunt freely. This he was not so sure about, but he eventually gave in on one condition: the land could be no greater than the area around which the girl could walk barefoot from now until sunset. She pleaded to be allowed sandals, but he refused.

So she started off at a brisk pace, first up the neighbouring hillside and then across the undulating hilltop, but thorns and brambles slowed her down and made her feet bleed. She struggled on the hilltop as far as she dared in the limited time she had been given, and then made her way down to the sea. At last, just before sunset she reached a point by the castle where the old farmhouse stands today. The route she travelled was carefully marked by following soldiers and became common ground. It is now known as Southerndown Common and has belonged to the people ever since.

The De Londres family were descended from one of the legendary twelve knights of the Norman conquest of South Wales. They were the lords of Ogmore and lived at Ogmore Castle.

THE ROMANTIC LEGENDS OF THE MAIDS OF SKER AND CEFYN YDFA

I apologise for having bundled these two great stories together so unceremoniously. The reason why will become clear, but in a nutshell, even though one is from the eighteenth century and the other from the nineteenth century, they are pretty much exactly the same story. This suggests that behind them both is a much older legend, one that gets retold every couple of generations, each time with a new set of well-known local lovers cast in the lead roles.

BUGEILIO'R GWENITH GWYN & THE MAID OF CEFN YDFA

I mentioned in my introduction that I have personal connections with some of these legends, and this is a case in point. In the late 1970s and 80s, as a boy I spent a great deal of time playing in the ruins of the great fifteenth-century manor house at Cefn Ydfa (*pronounced Kevun Ed-va)* and latterly inside the renovated house, which a good friend of my father's had been responsible for rebuilding.

Given my personal connection, I will begin by focussing on the Maid of Cefn Ydfa, the older of the two stories and the inspiration of the hauntingly beautiful Welsh folk song 'Bugeilio'r Gwenith Gwyn', which translates as 'Watching the White Wheat'. If you are not familiar with the song, I would highly recommend a quick trip to YouTube to hear it.

These are the words of one version of the song, as originally written in Welsh. There are other variants of this:

'Mi sydd fachgen ieuanc ffôl
Yn byw yn ôl fy ffansi,
Myfi'n bugeilio'r gwenith gwyn,
Ac arall yn ei fedi.
Pam na ddeui ar fy ôl,
Ryw ddydd ar ôl ei gilydd?
Gwaith rwy'n dy weld, y feinir fach,
Yn lanach, lanach beunydd.

Glanach, glanach wyt bob dydd,
Neu fi yn wir sy'n ffolach;
Er mwyn y Gŵr a wnaeth dy wedd
Dod im' drugaredd bellach.
Cwnn dy ben, gwel acw draw,
Rho im' dy law wen dirion;
Gwaith yn dy fynwes bert ei thro
Mae allwedd clo fy nghalon.

Tra fo dŵr y môr yn hallt,

A thra bo gwallt yn tyfu,
A thra fo calon dan fy mron
Mi fydda'n ffyddlon iti;
Dywed imi'r gwir heb gêl,
A rho dan sêl d'atebion,
P'un ai myfi ai arall, Ann
Sydd orau gan dy galon.'

This loosely translates into English as follows – with apologies in advance to any Welsh speakers who might find it easy to pick holes in this translation.

'A simple youthful boy am I
Who loves at fancy's pleasure:
I fondly watch the blooming wheat,
While another reaps the treasure.
Oh! Wherefore still despise my suit,
Why sighing keep thy lover?
For some new charm, thou matchless fair,
I day by day discover.

Each day reveals some newborn grace,
Or does fond faith deceive me?
In love to him who formed thy face,
With pity now receive me,
Then lift thine eyes, one look bestow.
Give me thy hand, my fairest,
For in thy bosom, lovely maid,
My heart's true key thou barest.

While hair adorns this aching brow

Still I will love sincerely,
While oceans roll their briny flow
Still I will love thee dearly.
Then tell the truth, in secret tell,
And under seal discover,
If it be I or who is blest
As thy true heart's best lover.'

This song and these words are said to have been written by a Welsh bard and poet called Wil Hopcyn (*pronounced Will Hopkin*). He was a peasant who earned a living as a thatcher in the village of Llangynwydd, near Maesteg. The words capture his feelings of love for a local girl he is forced to worship from afar, as their social circumstances keep them separated.

The girl in question is Ann Thomas. She was born in 1704 to a wealthy landowner, William Thomas, who lived at the nearby ancient manor house at Cefn Ydfa. Two years after her birth, her father tragically died, so Ann (the maid of Cefn Ydfa) was placed in the wardship of Anthony Maddocks, a wealthy lawyer from Cwm Risca Farm, near Bridgend, who had looked after her father's affairs. Maddocks had long planned that she would one day marry his son, who was also called Anthony. However, much to everyone's consternation she instead fell in love with the penniless poet and thatcher Wil Hopcyn. When this romance was discovered, Ann was imprisoned in her room at the manor. The Thomas and Maddocks families were both determined that her rightful suitor was Anthony Maddocks.

What they had not banked on was how deeply in love the pair were, and how determined they were to be together. They continued their relationship by writing love letters and poems to each other in secret. Ann would have hers delivered by a servant girl when she was running errands to the village. Wil would post his replies in the hollow of an oak tree on the Cefn Ydfa estate.

When this was discovered, Ann's mother confiscated all her writing materials. So desperate was Ann to communicate with her lover that she was said to have plucked leaves from the tree outside her bedroom window and written love letters to him in her own blood.

Records show that Ann Thomas married Anthony Maddocks 4th May 1725. Knowing the hopelessness of the situation, Wil Hopcyn moved away from the area, and Ann is said to have pined so heavily for her lover that she became very ill. On her deathbed she sent for him. He came running to her side, and on his arrival, they embraced, and she died in his arms of a broken heart.

Ann Maddcoks died in 1727 and was buried 6th June of that year in the churchyard of St Cynwyd's church, Llangynywd. The churchyard is opposite the cottage Wil Hopcyn is believed to have lived in, which during my youth was a pub called the Corner House, where every Friday night the regulars used to sing 'Bugeilio'r Gwenith Gwyn' back to his spirit.

A cross dedicated to Wil Hopcyn stands outside the church gates. This epic story was made into a silent film in 1904, the folk song was incorporated by composer William Parry into an opera, and the tale has been a staple part of Welsh folklore ever since its first telling.

*

This cross outside the church gates in Llangynwyd commemorates Will Hopcyn, the bard. He lived in the house which stands behind the memorial.

THE MAID OF SKER

Anyone reading who is familiar with RD Blackmore's romantic novel *the Maid of Sker* must at this point be thinking, 'What is this idiot talking about? The maid of Cefn Ydfa story is nothing like *the Maid of Sker*!'

There is a very good reason for that. The characters, chronology and plot of the novel borrow nothing from the legend of the same name. In fact, the only things the two have in common are the name and the setting. Everything else is totally different.

Blackmore's novel is essentially a story about how David Llewelyn, a local fisherman from Porthcawl, discovers a little girl cast adrift in a rowing boat. Believing her to be of noble birth, he takes her to the nearby manor of Sker House. The story then focusses on his exploits at sea during the war with France and her life growing up.

The author would undoubtedly have come across the original legend, growing up as he did in Nottage Court in Porthcawl. His vivid descriptions of the desolate, windswept landscape leave no doubt that he knew Sker and its surroundings well.

The original 'Maid of Sker' first appears in Welsh in a story book called *Y Ferch o'r Scer*, which was translated into English by William Davies of Neath in 1806. It is claimed that the story originated from an air composed by a local harpist by the name of Thomas Evans. As is the usual way, the story has been further embellished by subsequent retellings

Sker House is a pretty dour place. It was originally built as a monastic grange by the Cistercian monks of Neath Abbey in the fifth century. Later, in the sixteenth century, it was converted into a manor house. In my youth it was made even more eerie by the fact that it was partially ruined, but since 2000 I have been delighted to see it given a new lease of life after extensive renovation. It stands desolate and isolated in an eternal face-off with the sea to the south and the sand dunes on all other sides. It rises up like a megalith from the vast beach in front of it and has what is often described as a foreboding sense of loneliness. Blackmore describes it aptly:

> 'this always was, and always must be, a very sad and lonesome place, close to a desolate waste of sands and the continual roaring of the sea upon black rocks.'

Such a creepy place makes a perfect setting for a romantic legend, even though the one I am about to tell is disputed, not least by the family it is about, although the characters themselves are indisputably real.

Isaac Williams of Sker had two daughters. The youngest, Elizabeth, was tall, beautiful and elegant, and she loved to dance. She lived for the annual *Mabsant* (festival of the saint) which took place every year at the Town Hall of Kenfig (part of that ancient building is now the Prince of Wales Inn in Kenfig). One of the traditions of the Mabsant was that a harpist would be brought in to play throughout the night for the younger members of the community to dance until dawn.

One especially popular harpist was Thomas Evans of the parish of Newton and Nottage, the man credited with writing the song that this legend is based on. The sight of the beautiful Elizabeth Williams, dancing so elegantly through the night, caught his eye and quickened his pulse. He was utterly transfixed with her, and to his joy she made it obvious that his attraction was reciprocated. By the time the sun rose in the morning they were lovers.

When Isaac Williams got wind of this courtship, he was furious. After all, he was a gentleman farmer and lord of the manor, and Thomas Evans was a mere carpenter. He could not possibly be considered a worthy suitor for his daughter, no matter how good a harpist he was. Undeterred, Evans hired a horse and carriage and rode out to Sker House at night, in the hope that he could persuade Elizabeth to elope with him. But his plan was scuppered when he woke the dogs, who started barking and gave the game away. In response Isaac refused to let Elizabeth leave the house, and she was kept a prisoner in her room under lock and key until she was married off to Mr Kirkhouse of Neath.

She never got on with the husband that had been forced on her, and always begrudged him and her father for breaking her heart. She never forgot about her first true love and sought him out wherever there was a Mabsant in the area. She would always find a way to contrive to meet him in secret. On one occasion they were even caught together by her husband. Eventually she could not take the pain of being without her true love anymore and died of a broken heart. She was buried 6th January 1776 in Llansamlet.

Thomas Evans pined for her for so long that he did not take a wife until he had turned fifty. He died in 1819 and is buried in Newton churchyard.

There are obvious parallels between these two stories, and it is difficult to know how much of either is true. It seems inevitable, though, that a much older tale of hopeless love between a rich man's beautiful daughter and an irresistible but lowly bard is one many bards must have enjoyed telling down the generations.

ANCIENT DRUID FESTIVALS AND CEREMONIES

We have a lot of tradition in South Wales that originate before the Roman invasion, in our distant Celtic and druidical past. What always astounds me is how much of it has survived into the modern day, or at least up to really recent history. And I'm not talking about little hangovers from the past like hanging mistletoe at Christmas – which has nothing to do with Christmas and everything to do with the druidical belief that mistletoe harvested from an oak on the winter solstice had incredible powers of magic. I mean things altogether more full blown.

THE MARI LWYD

In the 1970s the Old House Inn in the village of Llangynwydd (the village at the heart of the legend of the Maid of Cefn Ydfa) was run by friends of our family, and as a young boy I would visit them frequently. They lived in one of the oldest pubs in Wales, and in a dark cove at the base of a stone spiral staircase was one of the most terrifying sites I had ever seen in my life. It was a horse's skull, darkened with age, streamers and ribbons hanging from it, mounted on a coat stand around which billowed a big white sheet. It had me running, screaming into the pub, much to the amusement of those gathered in it (grownups can be rubbish at times!).

Ancient ceremonies dating back thousands of years survived until recent years as traditions and customs – a lot of them unique to Bridgend and the Vale.

What I had seen was the central prop from a ceremony that dates back into pre-history, one that was still being continued in Llangynwydd in my lifetime and, as far as I am aware, is still carried on in some quarters now. The ceremony is called the Mari Lwyd and in its most stripped-down form consists of a man with a horse's skull for a head walking from door to door on the night of Christmas Eve. The origins of this tradition are long forgotten but it was clearly one of those pre-Christian festivals which the new religion rebranded and adopted to help win over local pagans.

In the Middle Ages there was a living to be made traveling from village to village performing mimes and plays about religious festivals. The protagonists in these religious shows were known as 'mummers', and it was troupes such as these who, at Christmas time in every town and village in South Wales, would carry the Mari Lwyd from house to house. The event was hotly anticipated. There is even a row of cottages in Cowbridge called 'Christmas Cottages' because they had the responsibility of keeping the Mari Lwyd through the rest of the year.

When this became a Christian tradition, there were usually three mummers to carry the Mari Lwyd, representing the Virgin, Joseph and the baby Jesus. Gradually the religious aspect dwindled, and the protagonists became just 'the leader', a man with a horse's skull for a head standing under a white sheet, and his guide and accomplice who was called 'the sergeant'. The skull was buried throughout the year in order to whiten it, and then dug up in time for Christmas. Then it was festooned with ribbons and decorations, including in some instances precious stones, before being mounted either on a stick or as a hat on the leader's head. I have even heard of lanterns being lit inside the skull so light would shine through the eye and nasal sockets. The lower jaw was usually wired onto the main skull so it would flap as if talking or laughing as it was carried. The Mari Lwyd was usually accompanied by a large party of men and youths, often with flaming torches, following behind to watch the hilarious antics.

This was a very early form of revelry and comedy show rolled into one, and the leader and sergeant were usually chosen for their quick wit and ability to make up rhymes on demand. They would lark around like an oversized Punch and Judy show, knocking on every door and demanding hospitality. There was a ritual to how a householder should respond to the knock at their door. If the householder was wise, on the first knock he would keep the door barred. The assembled company would then burst into song, with a lament about the plight of the poor in winter. At the end of the song, the leader would once again knock and ask for food and drink for all assembled. The householder in response would plead poverty (ideally in song). There would then be a showdown where the leader would pit his wits against the householder with riddles. If the householder could not answer his riddle, then he had to let the party in. Food and drink would be passed around, and the Mari Lwyd would chase the women or any young children of the household. Sadly this last detail is one of the things that led to the decline of this quaint and good-humoured tradition; on occasion rough elements would infiltrate the revellers and use the Mari Lwyd as a ruse for ransacking and robbing people's houses.

The name 'Mari Lwyd' directly translates as 'grey mare', but there are conflicting accounts of what it signifies. It is believed to have some derivation from the Welsh 'Mair' meaning Mary, (but given how absolutely terrifying the creature looks, especially to a small boy, I think 'grey mare' might have the same derivation as 'the nightmare'). The festival as it was before Christianity is likely to have been a ceremony for gathering offerings to give to the Celtic god Epona, the god and protector of horses (from whom we get the word 'pony'). The other possibility is that it was a ceremony designed to scare away evil and malevolent spirits during the depths of winter, the thought process being that only once the malevolent spirits of winter lost their grip on the darkness could Bel start to wake. Who is Bel, I hear you say? Well, it's funny you should ask...

THE BELTANE ON NEWTON GREEN

It is widely believed that the druids had a summer festival dedicated to Bel (also known as Belenos or Belenus), the Celtic sun god and god of light. Every year, on the summer solstice, a ceremony was held in which a large bonfire (called the Beltane) would be lit in his honour, to praise him and ask for a good harvest. This practice continued throughout most of Wales right up until midway through the nineteenth century. In Porthcawl, licence to hold this festival was enshrined in a bylaw dating back to the reign of James I in the early seventeenth century. The ceremony, held on Newton Green, was also a means of assuring the future purity of the waters of the well of St John (which we have already discussed).

The ceremony was performed by nine men who would begin by turning out their pockets and stripping themselves of any metal or reflective objects, money or any trappings of earthly or material wealth. This extended to belt buckles, spectacles and wedding rings. It was an important part of the ceremony that nothing metallic could touch any part of the body of a protagonist. The men then marched out from their starting point, to gather wood from no more nor less than nine different trees. They would then return to the common and cut either one or two circles in the turf and lay the twigs and branches they had gathered crosswise in the circle. They would then set the fire, by rubbing together two bits of oak that had been kept over from the remains of the fire from the previous year.

Once the fire had caught, the next part of the ceremony involved the nine men drawing white-meal and brown-meal oatcakes from a bag. Everyone who drew a brown-meal oatcake had to jump through the flames of the bonfire. Those who had drawn a white-meal one would clap and applaud as they did so. Once the fire had burned out, the charred logs were carefully stored away to be used to start next year's fire.

HARBINGERS OF DOOM

Every culture has its own myths and superstitions about what happens when your time is up. It comes from a craving for control over the unknown realms of death. The ancient Celts and druids had many. Some of them were pretty simple; for example, anyone who cut down a juniper bush would die within the week. Others were rather more convoluted, such as those listed below.

Somehow, despite Pope Innocent VIII declaring all superstitions to be a sin in 1484, they never really died out. They were still widely believed in Welsh communities right up to recent times. You may even have elderly relatives who still believe in some of them today.

Dogs of death

I have already mentioned a legend about a sleeping drover who was visited by a fox claiming to be the spirit of Einon Ap Colwyn, and explored how, in Celtic mythology, a visit from a fox was often a warning of death. As you might expect, this bit of folklore leaked into everyday beliefs, and undergoing the process of transformation typical of superstitions, it led to many legends about ghost or spirit hounds that visited people to announce their impending doom. These legends were usually associated with bleak spots like Sker or Newton Burrows, near Porthcawl, or sometimes with crossroads.

One such crossroads used to be where the Bryn Owain pub (formerly the Loch Fyne fish restaurant) now stands on the A48 near Cowbridge. At one time, on this spot, the Roman Antonine road was crossed by the lane leading to St Hilary to the north and the lane leading to Aberthin to the south. These days the A48 Cowbridge bypass has completely changed the road layout, but you don't have to strain your imagination too much to see how it once would have been. There were gallows here for the best part of 300 years, and it was here that, amongst others, the mass murderer Cap Coch (from our first story) was hanged. No surprises, then, that this was a frequent sighting place of a spirit hound. If you saw its ghostly shape – or more usually heard it howling – you would be lucky to see through the next 24 hours.

Seen singly, a spirit dog usually meant there would be a sickness or plague. A pack, however, meant certain death. They were greatly feared, known as 'cwn annwn', which translates as 'hell hounds'.

One of these packs of hell hounds is associated with Robert Fitzhamon, seemingly never far removed from local legends, although this time the link is through a mistress to whom he gave lands in Glamorgan. She was beautiful but cruel and 'wicked', a great horsewoman who loved riding to hounds. On one particularly exhilarating hunt she quipped, 'If I cannot hunt in heaven then I would rather not go there.'

She kept up the hunting until the day she died. When her soul left her body, she was refused entry into heaven and was instead given a pack of spirit hounds to ride with for all eternity. She became known as Mallt-y-Nos by terrified villagers, who most commonly claimed to see her around Christmas time. A sighting invariably led to a death.

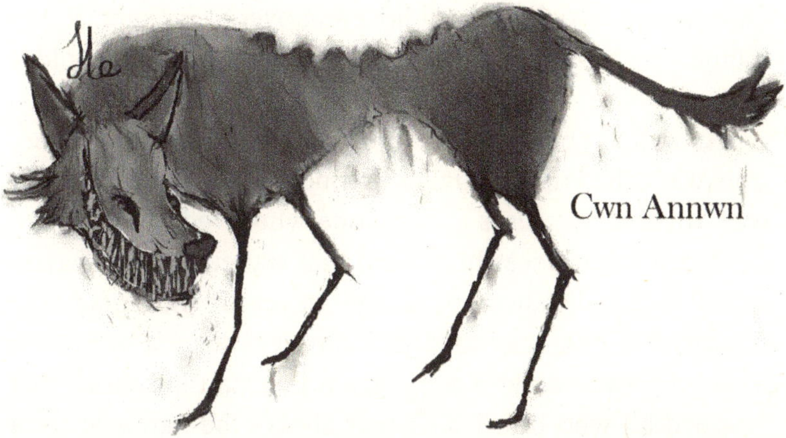

The Cwn Annwn started out as a legend about a hound which had strayed out of the spirit world into our own. By the eighteenth century it had become a superstition: a hell hound that haunted isolated spots, sightings foretelling impending doom.

DEATH KNELLS FROM THE SEA

A coastal area like ours is inevitably going to have lots of seafarer superstition and legend spun into its folklore. In fact, it is believed that the oft told seafarer's legend of Davy Jones' Locker, now known all over the world, has its origins amongst

Welsh sailors of the Bristol Channel, 'Davy' being an anglicised corruption of 'Dewi', which came about when the tale was retold by English sailors.

In addition to those salty tales you find across the shores of Britain, we have one or two that are quite unique to our area. One of these is the phantom lights of Tuskar. When the harbour was being built in Porthcawl, it was firmly believed that a ghostly light could be seen hovering above Tuskar Rock. Other times it could be seen hovering over Sker Point. It was thought by those who saw these lights that they foretold a coming wreck.

As well as phantom lights, we also had a phantom sound. This was called the 'cyhiraeth' (pronounced 'ku-hi-rye-th'). It was dreaded by sailors and anyone who lived near the sea, described as an unearthly sound that started off as a moan, heard in the distance across the waves. It then gradually increased in pitch and loudness until it became a scream. It might die away only to come again in a startling shriek that petrified all who heard it. It was always the harbinger of a terrible storm with the certainty of a shipwreck to follow.

We also had a number of quickfire superstitions that portended doom at sea. For example, if a man spat to the windward side before his outbound ship had passed Lundy Island, it would bring bad luck or death to a crew member. Or if a sailor noticed while sailing down the Bristol Channel that the sea at Nash Point roared louder than the sea at Breaksea Point, then the voyage was doomed.

The ship's cat, meanwhile, was a lot more than just a catcher of rats. He was a veritable barometer. If he mewed on board, trouble lay ahead. If he stretched out so his paws met before reaching Lundy (after leaving any port on the Bristol

Channel, it would seem) there would be storms. If more skittish than usual, it was a warning that there would be gales. If he frequently washed his face with the same paw, that was an omen of bad luck, and if he turned his back on the captain, the ship would be wrecked. Finally, if he sharpened his claws on the ship's mast all souls on board would be lost at sea with no hope of salvation.

CANWYLL CORFF – THE CORPSE CANDLES & PHANTOM FUNERALS

The legend of the 'canwyll corff' (*pronounced can-wool* corf), meaning corpse candle, is not unique to our area, but a concept that would be recognised in most parts of Wales. It was a ghostly light that would be seen to glow in the house of a person who was about to die. Sometimes the light was seen just in one room, sometimes the whole house. It also varied in colour: red for a man, blue for a woman or yellow for a child. There are even accounts of the light being a clearly visible, floating candle which passed from the house, over the route of the impending funeral or over a ship at sea.

If many candles were seen, it was a warning of an approaching epidemic. There are reports from the nineteenth century that in Bridgend, prior to an outbreak of smallpox, a host of canwyll corff were seen, warning that many people in the town would lose their lives to the disease. There is also an account of these spectral lights being seen above the pit head at Glyncorrwg before an explosion underground took the lives of several miners.

Sometimes witnesses would report manifestations of a

coffin with the candle floating over it, and, in some parts of Glamorgan, even entire phantom funeral processions. Usually, when these ghostly processions were witnessed, none of the protagonists could be clearly made out, only the coffin itself, or one distinctive-looking mourner. The procession would lead directly to the house of someone who was about to die.

Altogether there are loads of accounts of sightings. The following are just three of many.

In the mid-nineteenth century, a farmer from Llangynwyd was taking a horse and dray out to Porthcawl to collect fertiliser from the harbour, a journey he made fairly regularly. He would usually leave early in the morning to make sure that, even on the shortest days of the year, he could complete his journey before nightfall. On the day in question he set off from home around 4am, before dawn. He made good time, his route pretty much all downhill and the dray empty. He reported that he entered the outskirts of Porthcawl while it was still dark. Just as he neared a crossroads the horse stopped dead and refused to go any further.

In the gloom the farmer saw a crowd of people coming towards him. He could not make them out clearly, but as there was no street lighting back then, he thought nothing unusual of that. He reported that he could make out vague shapes and hear the shuffling of their feet as they came towards him. A coffin was carried past, followed by a man on a white horse, and then the procession wound its way out of the town.

Funerals do not generally take place in the dark, and intrigued, the farmer turned his horse and dray around and followed the cortege at a safe distance, just to satisfy his own curiosity. To his surprise he found himself being led back to Llangynwyd, where the coffin, the white horse and all the people just vanished.

Several weeks later a friend of his died and he found himself retracing the exact route he had taken on that early morning. Amongst the mourners was a man on a white horse. The farmer had seen the phantom funeral of his friend weeks before it actually happened.

There is a similar account of a Newton man who, possibly a little worse for wear, saw another such procession. Again, most of the mourners were no more than vague shapes, but one in particular caught his eye, a man wearing hunting pink (the red jacket worn by fox hunters). The procession passed him by but, instead of heading for the church, proceeded towards the inn he had not long staggered out of. Then it just disappeared.

The man told the pub landlord and anyone else who would listen about this ghostly funeral, but no one took his account very seriously. At least, not until a few years later, when the landlord of the inn died suddenly when on a trip to Neath. His body was brought back by road to the inn, where it rested prior to its burial in Newton Church's churchyard. In the funeral procession the next day, the most prominent mourner was a man dressed in hunting pink.

Our third account is from the beginning of the twentieth century. On a September evening a man was returning from Sker. The moon was very bright that evening, and he could make out the wreck of a huge vessel out at sea. A group of men were busily engaged wading out to bring something ashore. The man could not see exactly what it was but thought it looked like a coffin.

He watched as the men formed up on the beach, lifted the coffin to their shoulders and made off towards town. He followed to see where they were headed, and had quite a shock when the men halted outside his own front door. He broke into a run to catch them up, but as he reached them, they just vanished. He went indoors a bit shaken up and told his father what he had seen.

A week later there was a shipwreck off Sker point and among the drowned was the man's own brother, who had been away on a two-year voyage. The body was brought to the family home following exactly the same route the man had witnessed weeks earlier.

The tolling bell of Llantwit

There are many accounts of people in Llantwit Major being woken by the sound of a tolling bell in the dead of night. When they stepped out of their homes to investigate, they were surprised to hear that it was not emanating from the church tower of St Illtyd's, but apparently from a house in their neighbourhood in which no one had been stirred by the noise.

Within the week, someone in that house would be dead.

Twm, the prophet of Kenfig

Twm (Thomas) lived in Kenfig, possibly in the thirteenth century, and was said to have had the gift of prophecy. Specifically, he could foretell with staggering accuracy the time and manner of someone's death. Even as a young man he seemed to have a real gift, although it was one that, perhaps understandably, piqued the suspicions of the authorities and for a time led to his imprisonment in the castle at Kenfig.

Among the locals who were still talking to him after his release, he became a bit of a legend. One of his landmark predictions was when he foretold that the infant son of a local noble would die from strangulation. At first everyone ridiculed this, as the infant's parents were known to be both loving and protective. But those criticisms were soon stifled when the infant died, suffocated by his mother's own apron strings.

Twm's most famous prophecy, though, was when he told a local youth that he would die three times before the night. Again, everyone thought this was ridiculous. How could someone die three times? Later that same day, the boy went bird nesting and climbed a tree near the river Kenfig. When reaching out for the eggs he was bitten on the arm by an adder. He then fell and broke his back on a branch before finally plunging into the river, where he drowned.

Like I said. Uncanny.

GHOSTS OF BRIDGEND AND THE VALE

You cannot cover myths and legends without a small foray into ghost stories and tales of the supernatural. If you have a favourite one which I have left out of this section, then I must apologise. The reality is that pretty much every recognisable old building, road or landmark in South Wales has at least one, or quite often several stories attached to them. As most of them are broadly similar, I don't really see the point of cataloguing them all, and I will focus instead on the ones that are either very well known or particularly interesting. Outside of these, most fall into one of these three categories:

> Every pub over 100 years old claims to have a ghost in period dress who either slams doors, moves chairs or breaks glasses. Sometimes all three. Other than that, they tend to just sit in a specific chair.

> Every castle or manor house has the ghost of a maid who was mistreated by the master or a prisoner who died in custody there.
>
> Every crossroads has a ghost or a malevolent spirit.

A maid being abused by the lord of the manor is actually a recurring theme in ancient Celtic legends. As a story it predates any of the buildings it is attributed to today, so in a way, I am glad to see it being kept alive – likewise, people who died in captivity using their haunting to exact revenge.

Crossroads are an interesting one. There are no tales from the ancient Celtic world where crossroads play a central part. Is there predominance in ghost stories today to do with Christian sensibilities around the sign of a cross? It could be part of it, but it is more likely to be that, from the fourteenth to the nineteenth centuries, crossroads were genuinely scary places.

First of all, as I have said earlier, they were the traditional site of the gallows and, therefore, of executions. The place where notorious criminals and lowlifes met their end was bound to chill the blood of many a wary traveller, especially if, as a pious Christian (which most decent folk were back then), you believed that these men's deeds in life would have precluded their tortured souls ever finding rest.

Crossroads were also good places for outlaws to mount ambushes, offering four escape routes and plenty of cover. One account of such an assault comes from a letter written by a young lady of Llanblethian in the eighteenth century. She tells a rather grizzly story about some poor traveller, a packman from Scotland, who was beaten to death by bandits at the crossroads at Stalling Down, a place linked to multiple hauntings. The body was initially left by the roadside, a distressing sight for passersby of all ages to see, especially children.

People of the parish became very concerned, and efforts were made to identify somebody who might have known the victim, but no one was found. As such there was nobody in the parish to pay for a proper Christian burial. The solution they found was to roll the corpse into a ditch at the side of the road to rot. The writer of the letter was a churchgoer and very upset that the poor fellow would not have his soul handed over to God. She also wrote that, for months after, the stench was unbearable for passers-by.

If you witnessed something like this, at any age but especially as a child, it would hardly be surprising that from then on the crossroads might be a place you associate with dread, fear and evil. And for all its grisliness, this incident would not have been an experience unique to the area. Such occurrences doubtless would have contributed to the crossroads being seen as hotbeds of haunting and the supernatural.

THE WHITE LADY OF EWENNY

As a young boy growing up near Ewenny, I heard many accounts of the ghostly white lady, made all the more scary by the fact they were recounted by adults as much as my own age group. I did not realise until I was older that her haunting was so well known that it had a legend attached to it. I have also read that there is both a White Lady's Lane and a White Lady's Meadow on the marshland between Ewenny and

Bridgend (although I have never come across either personally). Many reports have been made of her apparition, and in those accounts, she is always described as looking anguished and forlorn. She is usually seen wringing her hands restlessly or pointing towards Ewenny. Some have speculated that she is pointing towards buried treasure.

The white lady of Ewenny is a ghostly spectre which many have reported seeing down the centuries. Some believe she is pointing to buried treasure; others say that her haunting is penance for a wicked life.

The most commonly retold story is that one day a man was crossing the marsh to the south of Ewenny Priory when he spotted her. As usual she was wringing her hands with a mournful expression on her face. Somehow, he plucked up the courage to speak to her and asked if he could help in any way. She turned to him and asked if he would hold her tight by her wrists and not let go on any account until she told him to. The man, though frightened, obliged, and as she held out her arms in front of her, he gripped them in his hands. But at just that moment the sound of a nearby dog barking startled him and he inadvertently lost his grip. The white lady's face twisted up in anger and she let out an unearthly scream, shouting, 'Now I shall be bound for another seven years!' Then she vanished.

Somewhat shaken he ran to the village and gave his account to some locals, who told him that the white lady was the spirit of a woman who was tormented by some terrible misdeeds from the past.

GHOSTS OF OGMORE CASTLE

The chap who encountered the white lady at Ewenny ought to be grateful that it was *this* white lady he ran into. A much older but less frequently sighted white lady is said to haunt the remains of Ogmore Castle, just a few miles away. Only this one is meant to have talons instead of hands, and is capable of severely mauling a fully grown man. One man at least is supposed to have died from wounds she is alleged to have inflicted, if not from the fright.

She may or may not be the same ghost frequently connected with a legend of treasure buried in the vicinity of Ogmore Castle, said to be guarded by a ferocious ghost. On one occasion the buried treasure was discovered by a local man who had heard about the legends. No sooner had it been lifted from the ground than he was met by the spectre of a ghostly woman, her face contorted with fury, who lashed out at him. He died of a fever within a few months of the incident.

It is probably not a coincidence that these two white spectres are associated with places that both belonged to Maurice De Londres. This leads me to believe that, somewhere, there is probably a story that links him and these ladies. I am sorry to say, however, that as yet I have not been able to find it.

There is also a legend that if you fall asleep on the banks of the river by the castle, you will wake up either in the past or in the future. Although given all these ferocious ghosts pottering about the place, who on earth would want to fall asleep there?

GHOSTS OF SKER

We have already spoken about Sker House, not least about its bleak and, frankly, creepy surroundings. Given its setting, it should be no surprise that it has its ghost stories as well. As you would expect, one of them is said to be the maid of Sker herself, Elizabeth Williams. Her ghost haunts the upstairs room where she was imprisoned by her own father, and her appearances are always heralded by the sound of clanking chains.

But there are other hauntings associated with Sker House too. During the Reformation, the owners refused to convert to the Church of England and continued to hold mass led by a Catholic priest. As this was a very dangerous practice, there are several hides and priest holes in the house, where clerics could be hidden away if the authorities came calling. One of them runs the length of a room on the other side of a false wall, and could be accessed from a hidden conduit up the chimney. This was called the Abbot's Walk, and in the middle of the night the ghost of a monk is meant to emerge from it, emitting tormented groans.

Outside the house things are just as busy. There can be found another very infamous spectre, known as Gwrach y Rhibyn, which rather cruelly translates as 'the hag of the mists'. She is a lost soul who wanders the dunes between Sker and Kenfig, uttering terrible cries. There is also the ghost of a white horse that haunts the same stretch of dunes. Legend has it that if you see it you will not live beyond the next twelve months – a belief that perhaps explains the presence of another white horse to be seen in the lanes around Llangynydd, as explored in the previous chapter.

Besides these white horses we have a few accounts of other ghostly animals in the locality. The famous spirit dogs of Glamorgan, explored in an earlier chapter, have been seen at Stalling Down near Cowbridge, the crossroads between Bryntirion and Laleston near Bridgend, and in the nineteenth century, the ghost of a postman's dog was reported walking with some urgency at the crossroads on the Ewenny-to-St Brides road, where the road towards Ogmore begins. Someone tried to pursue him, but he just vanished.

I have also heard told the tale of the ghost of a playful black dog who haunts the stretch of sand that appears during low tide between Barry Island and the Knapp. Apparently, he skips and plays with other dogs as they walk with their owners along the beach, then vanishes into thin air.

*

GHOSTS OF DUNRAVEN

We looked earlier at the story of the ship wreckers of Dunraven Castle and the final tragedy that befell Walter Vaughan. It is said that, on the night of the anniversary of his son's death, the ghost of Walter Vaughan stands at one end of Dunraven beach while the ghost of his son stands at the other. Walter looks mournfully towards his son and raises his arms to beg for forgiveness, but his son turns away from him with contempt and disdain before vanishing. Walter's ghost then lets out an anguished cry before vanishing himself.

CEFFYL D R

Another equine spirit is the ceffyl dŵr (pronounced ke-fill duw-er), which translates into English as 'water horse'. It is not unique to our corner of South Wales, but a character that infiltrates folklore throughout the Celtic world, including not just Wales but also Northumbria, Cornwall, Breton, Ireland and parts of Germany. Fundamentally it was a ghost horse, which frequented fords and river crossings, grazing on a nearby riverbank. An unsuspecting traveller, rather than getting his feet wet, would mount the ceffyl dŵr to cross the river. But at this moment the ghost horse would show its true colours. It would soar into the air, far above the ground, the terrified rider gripping its mane for dear life. The ceffyl dŵr would climb higher and higher until, at a few hundred feet off the ground, it would just vanish, leaving its mount to plummet to his death.

As you would expect, there was meant to be one which frequented the banks of the river Ogmore.

BWCI BO

The Bwci Bo was the name given to a race of goblins. They usually lived on farms or in the gardens of country cottages, out of sight but alongside their human neighbours. This creature used to strike fear into the hearts of children and adults alike, and superstition dictated that steps needed to be taken to placate them. The most common way was to leave a pail of milk outside the house every night. As long as this was done, the Bwci Bo would be content and leave you alone. In fact, legend has it that sometimes he might even do you the odd good turn, like curing an ill calf or lamb that otherwise would not have made it through the night. Occasionally, it might even tidy up the house while everyone was asleep!

However, if you did not keep them happy, the Bwci Bo had a very unpleasant side. If spied upon or ill-treated, they would turn nasty and bring bad luck on the house.

The Bwci Bo was often used as a bogeyman to scare children who did not do as they were told. 'If you don't tidy up your bedroom this minute, I will go out into the garden and call in the Bwci Bo!' would get little legs pumping up the stairs quicker than anything else known to man.

RAF AIRMEN

These are new stories to me. I only came across them for the first time when researching this book.

In June 2005 a father and son were walking home across Stormy Down when they were stopped in their tracks by the apparition of a ghostly airman in World War Two RAF uniform. From the movement of his feet, he was clearly walking, but as far as father and son could make out, he was not moving any closer. The airman then stopped, reached down to pick something up off the ground and disappeared.

Other people have claimed to see the ghost of an airman in this vicinity, nearby what was used as Hangar One, part of an RAF airbase in use throughout much of the Second World War. Some even report the sounding of a ghostly air raid siren.

In 2012 a shadowy figure was caught on camera in the area, and there is another spectre that has been snapped at the abandoned airbase just down the road at Llandow. This one got a lot of press coverage and can easily be found on the Internet. Its photo is believed by the photographer to capture a ghostly airman hiding in a bunker.

Also in Llandow, on 19th August 2009, a father and son were walking along the disused runway on a misty morning when they noticed a red flashing light on the control tower. The wind suddenly picked up, and as the mist cleared, there above them was the silhouette of a four-engine Second World War bomber, moving silently while banking over the airfield.

Musical ghosts

Earlier I dismissed a lot of pub ghosts as basically the same story retold over and over again, but here's a couple that are a little bit different.

We have mentioned in previous chapters that the Prince of Wales pub in Kenfig incorporates part of the building that was once the town hall of the lost city of Kenfig. So a ghost story probably would be on the cards. But in a strange twist, the ghost at the Prince of Wales plays the organ.

In the 1980s the landlord reported hearing phantom music, and a team of paranormal investigators came to the pub and set up recording equipment. The tapes definitely picked up something, but what those sounds were is not conclusive.

In another pub, the Castle Inn in Maesteg, the landlady was thought to have been murdered by her husband. Her ghost now creates cold spots throughout the pub, is frequently seen at the bar and whistles through the night to terrified guests.

A GHOST WITH A FASHION STATEMENT

Finally, a nice quirky ghost story to finish up. In Llantwit Major, in the early twentieth century, the ghost of a woman in high heels was often seen walking by 'the Ham', a large house owned by the Nicholl family on the road to St Donats. When building alterations were made at the house, a pair of high heeled shoes, identical to those the apparition had been seen wearing, were found encased within one of the walls.

DRAGONS OF THE VALE

If I was to tell you that there have been documented sightings of dragons in the area, you would more than likely imagine I was talking about an account from the Middle Ages, or maybe just before the Roman invasion. Not the early 1900s. But indeed, that is what I am about to share with you. And not just one report, *several* reports, from two villages, seventeen miles apart in the Vale of Glamorgan.

To put that into some kind of context, it is worth pointing out that at the turn of the twentieth century there was a very fashionable movement of belief in the occult and the supernatural. Even Sir Arthur Conan Doyle, the famous author of the Sherlock Holmes stories, was in on it. One of the most famous manifestations of this movement was a celebrated hoax called the Cottingly Fairies, where a series of doctored photographs were published, which purported to show real fairies living at the bottom of the garden. Many people unquestioningly accepted them as genuine, such was the appetite for proof that these things were real.

Evidence of such enthusiasm in our own area comes with our first account, from people who worked in the village and on the estate at Penllyn Castle, near Cowbridge in the Vale of Glamorgan. Those who are familiar with the area will know that the castle nestles in a great wood, on an outcrop which gently slopes down through the village to the Antonine road to the west, with a sheer drop to the east, overlooking a vast plain.

Dragon country: the castle and woods at Penllyn were reported as the home of a small colony of dragons in the late nineteenth century.

People had claimed to have been terrorised by 'dragons' or 'winged serpents' living in the woods around Penllyn Castle for many years. These creatures, though only the size of a dog, could turn unpleasant if provoked, and were a scourge of local farmers, a 'terror in the farmyards' and 'as bad as foxes for poultry'. In the account of an elderly villager, which was taken at the end of the nineteenth century, he describes them as 'winged serpents' and claims that he had seen them regularly since he was a small boy, claiming that they were beautiful things. They coiled when in repose and had brightly coloured scales which 'looked as if they were covered in jewels of all sorts. Some of them had crests which sparkled with all the colours of the rainbow.' If they were disturbed, they glided swiftly away to their hiding place 'sparkling all over'. If you made them angry, though, they 'flew over people's heads with outspread wings, bright and sometimes with eyes too, like the feathers in a peacock's tail'.

He made it quite clear that this was a genuine report and 'no old story to frighten children'. He even claimed that in the past his father had killed some, as they were such a nuisance for taking livestock. The interesting thing is that other people in the village backed him up.

There was also a similar account taken from a woman who, as a young girl, used to visit Penmark, near Barry. In her account, she said that she had often heard local people talking about 'ravages of the winged serpents' in the area. She described them in startlingly similar terms to the old man in Penllyn but went on to describe a social hierarchy amongst the beasts, claiming that each colony must have had a king and queen at its core. She also said that an old lady she used to know in the village had claimed that these beasts were guarding buried treasure and would remain docile unless it was ever discovered.

The following extract is quoted directly from her account

of how her grandfather and great uncle once hunted and killed one of these creatures. This was recorded by Marie Trevelyan in her 1905 book *Folk-lore and folk stories of Wales*:

> 'Her grandfather told her of an encounter with a winged serpent in the woods near Porthkerry Park, not far from Penmark. He and his brother "made up their minds to catch one and watched a whole day for the serpent to rise. Then they shot at it, and the creature fell wounded, only to rise and attack my uncle, beating him about the head with its wings." She said a fierce fight ensued between the men and the serpent, which was at last killed. She had seen its skin and feathers, but after the grandfather's death they were thrown away. That serpent was as notorious "as any fox" in the farmyards and coverts around Penmark.'

It is worth pointing out that these two accounts were both captured independently of each other and with neither party knowing the other.

Even now, there are people who believe that 'dragons' have always lived among us, claiming that dinosaurs never fully died out, just became rarer. In 1742 the essayist Owen Charles wrote this in *An Essay Towards a Natural History of Serpents*:

> 'among Serpents, we find some that are furnished with Wings. Herodotus who saw those Serpents, says they had great Resemblance to those which the Greeks and Latins call'd Hydra; their Wings are not compos'd of Feathers like the Wings of

> Birds, but rather like to those of Batts; they love sweet smells, and frequent such Trees as bear Spices. These were the fiery Serpents that made so great a Destruction in the Camp of Israel... The brazen Serpent was a Figure of the flying Serpent, Saraph, which Moses fixed upon an erected Pole: That there were such, is most evident.'

Could these creatures have been the dodos of Wales, dragons that lived among us only to be hunted to extinction by farmers protecting their livestock? Alas, we will never know.

THE ENCHANTED RIVER OGMORE

In pagan times, every waterway, from the smallest mountain spring to the vast estuary of the Severn, had a water spirit or god associated with it. As water is so fundamental to life, in their time these spirits were highly revered. But after Christianity took hold of the people of South Wales, these beliefs waned. In most cases they were either completely forgotten about or reduced to a handful of legends and superstitions.

Belief in the magical properties of the Ogmore, however, were widely held by locals throughout history, even until the nineteenth century. I must confess that even as a small boy growing up in the 1970s, when I used to walk my dog to the dipping bridge every day after school, I always felt as if the river had some soothing, ethereal quality about it. The riverbank always seemed to be the perfect place to get lost in childhood thought and daydream.

*

The river Ogmore has many legends, from buried treasure to mythical beasts, with magical powers abounding in every drop.

CHANGING THE WAYS OF THE 'BAD MEN'

Once Ogmore Castle had ceased to be a baronial court, the area around the estuary of the Ogmore became rather desolate and forgotten. Taking advantage of its remoteness, during the rather lawless eighteenth century a band of outlaws had their hideout in the area. Like many bandits we have already talked about, they made their living as highwaymen, preying on lone travellers and packmen, and also salvaging from shipwrecks, with all the skulduggery attendant with that grisly profession. There is also a possibility that they were associated with kidnapping. A local belief held that a family of water ogres lived in the Skee Well near Ewenny. Legend has it that they would carry off young maidens who lingered too long by the well, imprisoning them in the springs that fed it. Any reports of missing girls would most likely have been blamed on the ogres rather than this bunch of cutthroats, who were, in my opinion, altogether more credible suspects.

One day, the springs which fed all the wells along the Ewenny and Ogmore estuaries ran dry. These were the principal sources of fresh, clean drinking water for both bandits and locals alike. It was claimed that, if you listened at the wells, you could actually hear the springs 'groan'. At the same time, the principal food source of the area, the fish in the rivers, all disappeared, and instead its waters teemed with venomous snakes and toads. The local people became convinced that the actions of this merciless band of ruffians had angered the water spirits of the Ogmore, and this was their punishment. So a couple of brave locals approached the leader of the gang to share their concerns. The gang, being just as superstitious, took the advice offered to them and went to the wells to tell the water spirits that they were truly sorry for how they had behaved, and made a vow to change their ways. Within a few days, the springs had responded, and water gushed forth, filling all the wells, and the snakes and toads once again gave way to a bounty of fish in the river.

The bandits, realising the importance of their vow, planted trees around the wells to provide shade for the people who visited them, and gave up their lives of crime, turning instead to honest labour on the land.

BURIED TREASURE

There is a widely held belief that in addition to boasting magic powers, the Ogmore is also guarding buried treasure. From this spun a plethora of related ghost stories, either of spectres showing people where the treasure is or killing anyone who would try to take it (such as the white ladies in our previous chapter). There were also legends of ghosts who haunted the banks of the Ogmore, lamenting that they had died before being able to retrieve treasure they had buried either in it or along its banks. These tormented souls were unable to rest until the treasure was found. The only way to free their souls was to find their treasure and then return it to the river downstream. One such ghost story is set in the village of Newton, two miles west of the Ogmore estuary.

In the latter part of the nineteenth century, there were sightings of the spectre of a tall, gaunt man wearing clothes from a previous age. He had a mournful facial expression and would point to the dunes at Newton Burrows. One day he appeared to a man walking on the beach whose courage may have been fortified by some cwrw da (Welsh for 'good ale'). He plucked up enough courage to approach the apparition and ask what was the cause of his apparent misery. The ghost beckoned and led the way to a spot in the middle of the dunes, signalling for him to dig at a specific point. Well, dig he did and after shifting about two feet or so of sand, he found a wooden box. He cleared enough sand around it to be able to pull it out from its shallow grave and opened it. Inside were precious stones and metals, a really impressive haul of treasure by anyone's standards.

Loyal to the dictates of legend, he took the box to the river Ogmore and tossed it into the river downstream. From that moment on the ghost was never seen again.

There were numerous other superstitions associated with the river. One of my favourites was that, if a maiden wanted to see who she would marry, she had to take an item of underwear and soak it in the waters of the river. She then had to carry it home without touching it so would carry it in her teeth. Once home it had to be placed by the fire to dry. Then, before her very eyes, the face of her future husband would appear before her in spirit form, only disappearing if the garment was touched by hand or turned around.

Before crossing the river on foot, it was also customary to spit three times, else run the risk of being swept downstream to your death in a sudden surging current.

PART THREE

CUSTOMS, SUPERSTITIONS AND REMEDIES

REMEDIES AND MEDICINES

In prehistoric times, if you were ill, you would seek out the village druid. He would have the magic spell or potion that would see you back to health. But that was how it was done thousands of years ago, so you might expect druidical remedies to be nothing but a footnote in the ancient history books. In reality, however, medicine in its traditional sense was not widely available to ordinary people until the twentieth century. Before that, only rich people could afford to see a physician, and even then, by modern standards remedies were more than a little suspect.

Accordingly, even though after the introduction of Christianity druids lost their roles as high priests, for a millennium they retained their place as medics. They finally disappeared in the fourteenth and fifteenth centuries, when the church got a bit twitchy about witchcraft, and it became likely that anyone claiming to heal through any means other than the name of Christ was likely to meet a sticky end. However, even after the last druid doctors were gone, their practices, ceremonies and recipes were passed down the generations by word of mouth.

As the ones who generally ended up with the responsibility of caring for the sick, they were generally the reserve of the women of the family. This is why accusations of the practise of witchcraft were, more often than not, levelled at women rather than men.

So many of our customs and superstitions have their origins in pagan druidical traditions that go back thousands of years.

You might think that the introduction of the NHS would have spelled the end of these antiquated remedies. But let me share a true story with you. When I was about ten years old, in the late 70s, I noticed that I had developed a wart on my wrist. I happened to mention this to one of my friends of the same age in the playground. He suggested that I ought to rub it with a snail with a black shell and then nail the snail to a tree. When the snail rotted, the wart would be gone. I asked him how that worked? He replied he didn't know, but that he had done it and his wart had disappeared.

Let's back up a minute and really look at this. This advice was being dispensed at the tail end of the twentieth century, not by a grandmother born in a previous century, but by a ten-year-old boy in a playground. I have to confess that I didn't take his advice. Instead I went down the unconventional route of telling my mum, who took me to Boots to buy some curious potion which made the wart turn black and drop off.

What neither my friend nor I fully grasped was that the remedy he had suggested was as old as time. It was a traditional druidical remedy that had been employed by Celtic folk all over ancient Britain and beyond for over 2,000 years. And I am sure there are more recent examples of it being suggested, even employed.

Here is a list of common remedies I have encountered down the years, while growing up as a confused youth in South Wales. Some, but not all, are derived from ancient druidical traditions. Others became part of the repertoire of household cures in more recent history. You will find some of these amusing, some ridiculous, but I can guarantee there will be some reading through this section nodding their heads, saying, 'My mum used to say that!'

> Before dispensing any remedies, it was worth checking to see if the patient was ever likely to make a recovery. Nettles placed under the pillow were the best indicators. If by the morning the

nettles were still green, then your patient was at least in with a chance. If the nettles had already started to wither, then the end was already in sight.

Rosemary was a remedy for drunkenness.

Leeks or garlic rubbed on the body before battle or a fight would prevent wounds. The pugilists of the old bareknuckle boxing days used both.

Nettles boiled and eaten quickened the senses and, if taken at night as an infusion, would help you sleep more soundly.

Ivy had a multitude of applications. According to druidical tradition, it was endowed with magic from the tree spirits. As such, it was used to safeguard against sorcery and possession (which we believe today was a term most commonly used to describe schizophrenia). During smallpox epidemics, households would lock down for fear of contracting disease. However, milk maids still had to go out and milk the herds twice a day. To protect themselves, they wore ivy around their necks and wrists. No milk maid appeared to get any symptoms, so people concluded that these garments must be particularly effective. In reality, because of their regular contact with cattle, the milk maids were contracting the harmless strain of the virus called cowpox. This effectively inoculated them against the much more deadly strain that claimed so many lives.

Two cures for a headache: strike your head three times with a stone in a thunderstorm, in which case you will have relief for a year; or hold your head under water for a few seconds and pour melted tallow (whale fat) into the water through a carding comb. If the water is then thrown onto an elder tree and the tallow into the fire, the headache will be cured.

A person suffering from hiccoughs would be cured by drinking out of a jug over the handle.

Boils could be drawn by pressing them with crossed knives.

A horseshoe placed under a pillow eased convulsions.

If a woman was suffering from earache, she would wrap a man's breeches around her head.

Epilepsy could be kept at bay by wearing an amulet made from a coffin handle.

A new bride's wedding ring could cure a sty if it was drawn nine times across the infected eye. As a foot note to this, it is worth pointing out that the number nine was a sacred number to druids. You may recall that in the ceremony of the Beltane there were nine protagonists who gathered wood from nine trees. The Vikings also revered the number nine, having nine virtues of nobility and a belief that heaven and earth contained nine realms. Also, Odin hung himself from a tree in search of enlightenment, for nine days.

Seaweed poultices were a cure for ringworm.

Elderflower infusions are ideal for whitening skin. You may wonder why you would want your skin whitened at all, when in twenty-first century western culture many people crave a sun-bronzed complexion. Before the twentieth century, however, tanned skin was very unfashionable, indicating that you were a peasant who had been toiling on the land. The gentry would show off their pale complexions as evidence of a life kept indoors, in the lap of luxury.

Wine made from elderflower, meanwhile, was meant to help you sleep. I had a friend who used to make her own elderflower wine. It was so potent that it was more likely to induce paralysis than sleep.

Carrying a potato in your pocket was a sure-fire way of curing rheumatism. This belief is clearly not druidical in origin, as potatoes were not brought to Wales until the seventeenth century. It is worth adding that, when Sir Walter Raleigh first brought back potatoes and tobacco from the Americas, both were believed to possess incredible healing powers,

> not just in South Wales but throughout Britain.
>
> To cure rickets, you had to crawl under a blackberry bush.
>
> Red flannel next to the skin was a cure for rheumatism. Red blinds and bedclothes were an antidote for smallpox.
>
> Mayflowers gathered before sunrise and rubbed on the skin kept freckles away.
>
> To cure whooping cough a lock of the sufferer's hair had to be cut and put in a sandwich and fed to a dog. It was important to use a dog you were not too attached to, because once the dog had eaten the sandwich, he then needed to be evicted from the home. The whooping cough left with the dog.
>
> Finally, parsley was believed to be good for 'cleaning the brain'. When I first came across this one, I had no idea what 'cleaning the brain' meant. Then it came to me – it is the perfect remedy for a dirty mind!

Before I end this section, a final disclaimer from me: don't try any of these at home! I am no doctor, but I would not recommend putting them to the test. If you genuinely are suffering with any of the symptoms described, perhaps it would be best to consult a medical professional instead.

MAKING A HAPPY, HEALTHY HOME

These days, when we move to a new house, we talk about the importance of creating a happy, healthy home. In days past, just as important as happy and healthy was 'lucky'. Getting a new home blessed by a holy man is common in most cultures and has been going on in Wales since before Christianity. But the Welsh liked to be sure of good fortune, so in addition to a blessing, there was also a wealth of superstitions that were observed to make sure that a home and its family thrived. We can only guess where these all originate, but no doubt some date back thousands of years.

Fern hung in the doorway would keep the devil from entering the house. If you wanted to be doubly sure, the addition of dried seaweed would keep him firmly at bay.

Bringing mayflower into a house was believed to be unlucky. This probably originated from the battle of Bosworth Field, where King Richard III's crown was found in a hawthorn bush.

Rosemary laid under a threshold would prevent snakes from entering the home.

Wearing underclothes inside out kept witches away.

If a dove or crow hovered above a house it was a sign of impending disaster.

Lightning would never strike a house as long as there was a fire burning in the hearth. If you wanted to be extra sure, then two sheathed knives were to be lain crossed against a window.

If crickets suddenly deserted a house in summer, there would be a death in the family.

If you allowed tears to fall on the dead, they would have no rest.

A family moving into a new house at the new moon would have an abundance of food.

If you counted your money at the new moon your purse would never be empty.

It was considered dangerous for a child to sleep with the rays of the moon on its face.

During an eclipse the water in a well had to be

> covered, otherwise it would be contaminated by evil spirits.
>
> Putting shoes on a table would instantly bring bad luck.
>
> A person using a sewing needle on Good Friday would be struck by lightning.
>
> It was not all about the house either. There were also quite a few superstitions attached to the garden:
>
> If a pregnant lady did too much gardening, her child would lack a sense of smell. The baby should also not be given a rattle, as it would then be late talking.
>
> You were never to plant blackthorn and whitethorn side by side, otherwise they would disagree and bring bad luck to the planter.
>
> Two sayings to keep you and your household in good health: Cry before breakfast, laugh after supper (or vice versa); After dinner rest a while, after supper walk a mile.

When it's time to step outside the house, you always want to check the weather first – and if you think modern weather forecasts can be unreliable, imagine if all you had to go on were these superstitions:

When the fog came from the sea, the bees would make much honey. When it came from the hills the corn would be good and plentiful.
A stranger in the village would surely make it rain.

A misty May meant a hot summer.

If the froth on a tankard of ale spilled over on St Andrew's day, the year would be wet; if it stayed heaped on top it would be dry.

A green winter made for a full churchyard.

A fine February would mean a cold November.

The wetter the April the hotter the June.

A damp pantry in June meant a hot summer.

When Autumn bushes are heavy with berries we are in for a harsh Winter

Ice in December was a sure sign that clover would be out at Easter.

If it rained on Christmas Day, it would rain from May to May.

LOVE AND COURTSHIP

It's a timeless tale of boy meets girl. You know the rest, I'm sure. But as William Shakespeare put it, 'The course of true love never did run smooth.' Down the ages, our ancestors have sought out all the help they can get. Here is a collection of sayings and superstitions that South Wales lovers once employed to make sure that the course of love ran as smoothly as possible.

Most of these sayings and superstitions are very much from the female perspective. That does not mean that there were not male equivalents, only that I didn't find them in my research.

Firstly, it was important to know who the target of your affections should be. There were several methods to find that out. In our chapter dedicated to the magical properties of the river Ogmore, we spoke about the legend that, if a maiden were to wash an undergarment in the magical waters, her suitor would be revealed to her while it dried. All well and good if you lived an easy commute from the banks of the river, but what about everyone else?

Well, there was one solution that was popular amongst farmers' daughters down the ages. You needed to collect a handful of harvested onions, lay them lengthways on a windowsill and name each one after each of the local bachelors. The one which sprouted first was to be your betrothed.

If access to onions was also problematical, you still had an option available to you. It was said that if a girl went to bed on St Andrew's day without her nightdress on, the saint would show her a vision of her future husband.

There were a number of tactics you could employ if you wanted to be sure that the person you fancied was also attracted to you. If a girl was to wear the valerian flower under her bodice or girdle, it was guaranteed to draw admiration from the opposite sex. But if you thought you might need a love potion to make sure of their devotion, then using the myrtle plant in your ingredients was a must.

If the opposite was her intent, however, and a lady wanted to be sure of being left alone, she should wear a garter made of mountain ash bark. That would protect her from wandering hands.

If two girls broke a wishbone together (from a chicken carcass) the one with the bigger piece would be married first and the one with the shorter piece would be the first to have a child.

Oh, and one last tip from the ancient Welsh – if married in July, you will live to sigh.

PART FOUR

PLACE NAMES AND THEIR DERIVATIONS IN BRIDGEND AND THE VALE

WHAT'S IN A NAME?

I find place names fascinating, regardless of whether their meanings and origins are obvious or cryptic. They are a snapshot of a moment in time, frozen throughout history. They reveal the roots of the places around us. Who lived there, what happened there… And they are all around us. Obviously, the ones which fascinate me the most are the quirky ones. Ones that are a bit weird or that have a twist in the tale. Regardless, I must confess that, whenever I arrive for the first time in any place, my first thought is always 'I wonder why it's called that?'

Many local place names are just expressions of aristocratic vanity. All they tell us is the name of the family of most influence when the area underwent a period of expansion. We have a great example of that in Bridgend. As I have mentioned before, the town saw a period of rapid growth after the main London road got diverted through it in 1825. At that time, most of the town and surrounding land belonged to the Dunraven Estate, and the earls of Dunraven were the Wyndham family. For that reason, to this day we have a lot of street names dating back to that expansion, like Dunraven Place and Wyndham Street. Even the streets around them were named after the ladies of the family, such as Caroline Street.

Sometimes we get thrown curveballs, where a place name does not have the origins you might expect. One that used to mystify me was Llangynwyd. I used to think it meant 'church of progress', which is what it looks like if you translate it directly from Welsh to English. It made me wonder, what was so progressive about the church in Llangynwyd? It just goes to show that a little bit of knowledge can be a dangerous thing. It turns out that it's nothing to do with that. It's just that the village and church were founded in the sixth century by Saint Cynwyd.

Another one is Dinas Powys. To me, Dinas has always translated as 'city', which always seemed at odds with the fact that, as lovely as Dinas Powys is, it's hardly a buzzing metropolis. I also always assumed that the 'Powys' bit was a reference to the ancient Welsh kingdom which spanned mid-Wales. An altogether more plausible theory only got offered to me recently. 'Din' (as opposed to 'Dinas') does not mean 'city', it means 'hillfort', and 'Powys' in this instance is not derived from Welsh but from the Latin word 'pagus', meaning pagan. In other words, the village is named after the pre-Christian hillfort that is reputed to have stood at Cwm George, near the later Norman construction.

Most of our place names are Welsh, but every now and then you find one that was named by settlers or invaders from overseas.

Besides the Romans and the Normans, we haven't had many influxes from outside South Wales, especially when compared to somewhere like Pembrokeshire, which at different points in its history became the new home of many Irish, Danes, French Huguenots, English and Dutch. In comparison, we have only a couple of place names to evidence outside influence. For example, there were only one or two minor Viking settlement in our area, nothing like the numbers seen in other parts of the country, and especially low when you consider that, as mentioned in a previous chapter, we are so close to Swansea, which was the biggest Viking settlement in South Wales. That was established in the early eleventh century by Sweyn Forkbeard, and the name 'Swansea' is derived from the old Norse name 'Sweynse', meaning 'Sweyne's Island [or Inlet]'. We know that Steep Holm and Tusker Rock are both Norse in origin, as is Sker. We also have a few other possible candidates, in Norton and Nurston, both likely to be derived from 'Norse Town'.

The long-held wisdom is that Rhoose got its name from the Welsh word 'Rhiw', meaning a hill or a path that follows a steep incline. For example, Bridgend's shopping precinct the Rhiw is built close to where a steep stone staircase once climbed from the bottom of Caroline Street to the top of Nolton Street. In its day, it was the steepest incline in the town centre. However, if you stand in the oldest part of Rhoose and look around in any direction, you may notice a very gradual, mild incline, but nothing that would warrant the title 'Rhiw'.

Another possibility is that 'Rhoose' is derived from the Welsh word 'Rhos', meaning point or headland. After all, Rhoose Point is the southernmost tip of mainland Wales. The problem here, though, is that although today Rhoose and Rhoose Point are contiguous, this has only recently become the case. The oldest part of the village is more than a mile inland from the point, so why would it be named after it? And why would the Welsh name for the village be 'Rhws' not 'Rhos'?

Well, there is another theory I have been presented with, which suggests that it could be Norse.

In Constantinople during the Byzantine period, all traders who came and went through the city's bazaars had to sign a register to declare who they were, where they were from and what they were selling. The Viking slave traders were frequent visitors, and they referred to themselves as 'the Rus' (which is the Norse word for 'Viking'). It is from this derivation that the land they colonised to the east ultimately became called *Rus*sia. It is a speculative theory, but lending it credibility is the fact that Rhoose is located right next to the small hamlet of Nurston, itself most likely of Norse derivation, and also that a family who farmed in the area for many generations had the surname Odin, the Norse king of the gods.

You could be mistaken for thinking that 'Wick' sounds like it might be Norse, but it appears frequently in Saxon texts meaning 'farm'.

Sometimes place names tell of an event or legend long forgotten. The best example we have locally is Llancarfan, which means church of stags. If you read the chapter on miracles you will recall that there is a legend that two stags came out of the forest to help St Cadoc build the monastery at Llancarfan. We also have another place name based on a saintly legend. It is not as well-known as the Llancarfan one, and is a bit more contentious, but supposedly for a time St Cornelius, a very early saint, lived the life of a hermit in a cave in Cornelly, near Porthcawl. We don't know a lot about St Cornelius. We think he was French but know for sure that he is the patron saint of horned cattle. In parts of France, he is credited with starting a blessing ceremony of cattle that continues to be practised. His cave was said to have been somewhere near the entrance to the quarry, which is still in use today. His time in the area gave his name to the village.

Sometimes a place name started off as one thing and then, through repetition, ended up corrupted, or something crucial getting lost in translation. Earlier in this book we looked at the mysterious Roman town of Bomium. For that to have ever ended up as 'Cowbridge' then at some point Bomium must have become Bovium (which means cattle) before being translated to Cowbridge. There also used to be a village between Tythegston and Merthry Mawr called Candleston. It was lost to the sand dunes but is still known for the remains of the castle next to the car park at the start of the dunes in Merthyr Mawr. In reality Candleston Castle was never a castle in the strictest sense. It was a fortified manor house belonging to a family of Norman nobles called the Cantaloupes (which means 'running wolves'). This leads many to believe that the name Candelston is a corruption of 'Cantaloupe's Town'.

You also sometimes find place name patterns. For example, in the Vale of Glamorgan there are a lot of small villages named after saints such as St Hilary or St Athan. That is because, through history, a lot of land in the Vale was owned and managed by the monasteries at Llancarfan, Llantwit Major and Monknash. The same is true near Kenfig, where a lot of land was owned by the abbeys at Neath and Margam. It was traditional for them to name each of their farms after a saint of their order, in the same way public schools name their houses after celebrated alumni. The villages grew up around the farms and in time took their names.

Not all place names are interesting, I accept. In Wales we have over 500 place names beginning with the word 'llan', a Welsh word originally meaning 'meeting place' but more typically indicating a parish church. If 'llan' is followed by a saint's name then, I grant you, there's not much to get your teeth into. Similarly, you get a lot of place names that just describe a location, such as Bridgend – a town at one end of a bridge crossing – or Aberthaw, which is just Welsh for 'estuary of the river thaw'. I guess most people could have worked those out without looking them up in a book, and neither is likely to prompt a reaction of 'well fancy that'.

Of course, if you are not a Welsh speaker then Aberthaw might have seemed a bit trickier than otherwise. For the benefit of those not conversant in the language of heaven, here are some common Welsh words that crop up a lot in place names, followed by their English meaning. Some will be familiar from place names elsewhere in Europe. This is because some Welsh words have Latin origin, such as 'bont' or 'pont', meaning bridge, which is very close to the French. Others sound familiar because many Welsh words were shared by other ancient British dialects. For example, 'afon', which is Welsh for river, was commonly used by Anglo Saxons. As a result, there is more than one river in England called the Avon, which is simply an anglicised pronunciation of the same word.

Aber – Estuary, confluence, tributary, the end of a waterway
Afon – River
Allt – Wooded hillside
Bedd or the plural *Beddau* – Grave
Betws or *Bettws* – Chapel
Blaen or *Blaenau* – The source of a stream or spring
Bont – Bridge
Bryn – Hill
Bwlch – Mountain pass

Cae – Field or enclosure
Caer – Fort, castle or stronghold
Capel – Chapel
Carn or *Carnedd* – Similar to the Scottish word 'cairn' usually meaning an ancient burial site or tomb, or a mound or a pile of stones
Cas or *Castell* – Castle
Cefn – Hilltop or mountain ridge
Cei – Quarry
Cil – Corner or hideaway
Clog or *Clogwyn* – Steep cliff
Coed – Forest or wood
Craig – Rock
Croes – Crossroads or cross
Crug – Small hill or tump
Cwm – Valley (usually glacial)
Cymer – Where two waterways meet (confluence)
Din – Ancient hillfort
Dinas – City
Dol – Meadow
Dwr – Water
Dyffryn – Rolling valley
Eglwys – Church
Erw – Acre
Fach – Minor or small
Fawr – Major or big
Ffin – Boundary
Ffordd – Road or thoroughfare
Ffos – Ditch or trench (similar to the French word fosse)

Ffridd – Mountain pasture
Ffynon – Spring
Garth – Garden, pound or enclosure
Glan – Riverbank
Glyn – Deep valley
Gwaun – Scrub moorland
Hafod – Summer croft or smallholding
Hendre – Winter croft or smallholding
Llan – Meeting place or church
Llanerch – Clearing in a wood
Llyn – Lake
Maen – Stone
Mawr (same as Fawr) – Major or big
Melin – Mill
Merthyr – Martyr (usually a saint or someone who was killed for their Christian faith)
Mor – Sea
Morfa – Salt marsh
Mynydd – Mountain
Nant – Brook or stream
Newydd – New
Pant – Hollow
Parc – Park
Pen – Head or point
Pentre – Village
Plas – Hall or mansion
Pont – Bridge
Porth – Harbour or port but can also mean gate
Pwll – Pool
Rhiw – Hill or steep incline

Rhos – Moor
Rhyd – Ford or river crossing
Sarn – Causeway
Sir – County
Stryd – Street
Tafarn – Pub or Inn
Treath – Beach
Tref – Settlement
Ty – House
Ystrad – Valley floor

ACKNOWLEDGEMENTS

1 *Roman roads in Southeast Wales* – a report for Cadw by Andy Sherman BA and Edith Evans BA PhD MIFA

2 *Legends of Porthcawl and Glamorgan Coast* by Alun Morgan

3 *Hello Historia – The Woollen Factory* by Louvain Rees

4 The archives of *the Glamorgan Gazette*

5 *Romans in the Vale* by Karl-James Langford

6 *Excavations in Cowbridge 1977-88*, Parkhouse & Evans, 1996

7 *Roman & Medieval Wales* by CJ Arnold

8 *Dictionary of Welsh Biography*

9 *A Topographical Dictionary of Wales* by Samuel Lewis

10 *The Normans in Welsh History* by Huw Pryce

11 *Society of Cymmrodorion* by G Peredur Jones

12 *When Wales was a Smuggler's Haven* by Phil Carradice

13 *Llantwit Major – a Fifth Century University* by AC Fryer

14 *The Book of South Wales, the Wye and the Coast*, by SC Hall

15 *Owain Glyndwr – Prince of Wales* by RR Davies

16 *A Popular History of the Ancient British Church* by EJ Newell
17 Transaction from The Bristol and Gloucester Archaeological Society
18 *The Battle of St Fagans* by Ellen Castellow
19 *Caradoc of Llancarfan* by JSP Tatlock
20 *Butler's Lives of the Saints* by Alban Butler
21 *Wales & the Crusades* by Kathryn Hurlock
22 *Citizen of Cardiff* by Frank Hennessey
23 The Holy Bible
24 Paranormaldatabase.com
25 *Folk-lore and folk stories of Wales*, by Marie Trevelyan
26 'What's in a name' by BBC Wales
27 *The Vikings*, by Neil Oliver
28 English/Welsh Dictionary
29 Thanks to my step-brother Robert Williams for help with proof reading
30 Thank you to my amazing wife Belinda for her patience and for indulging me the time I took to research and write this book while jobs around the house were starting to stack up

DO YOU KNOW SOMEONE WHO WOULD LOVE THIS BOOK?

If you want to buy further copies of this book, we can offer some great discounts when you buy direct from the author. Simply visit our website for more information at:

https://www.bridgendvale.co.uk.

JOIN OUR COMMUNITY:

We like to keep our readers informed of local folklore and quirky stories as we discover them. You can keep up to date or contribute on any of our social media platforms:

Facebook: facebook.com/BridgendValeLegends

Twitter: twitter.com/@FolkloreOf

Instagram: Instagram.com/ bridgendandthevalelegends